MASSAGE
The Healing Power of Touch

Karen Smith

Commissioned photography: Antonia Deutsch

DUNCAN BAIRD PUBLISHERS

LONDON

Massage
The Healing Power of Touch

This edition first published in Great Britain in 2003 by
Duncan Baird Publishers
Sixth Floor, Castle House
75–76 Wells Street
London W1T 3QH

Conceived, created and designed by
Duncan Baird Publishers

Managing editors: Catherine Bradley, Judy Barratt
Project editor: Molly Perham
Managing Designer: Gabriella Le Grazie
Designer: Gail Jones
Photographic art director: Sue Bush
Picture research: Fiona Hill

British Library Cataloguing-in-Publication Data.
A catalogue record for this book is available from the British Library

ISBN 978-1-84483-699-4

1 3 5 7 9 10 8 6 4 2

Typeset in Gill Sans
Colour reproduction by Colourscan, Singapore
Printed in Singapore by Imago Publishing Limited

Publisher's note
Before following any advice or exercises contained in this book, it is recommended that
you consult your doctor if you suffer from any health problems or special conditions or
are in any doubt as to its suitability. The publishers, the author, and the photographer
cannot accept responsibility for any injuries or damage incurred as a result of following the
exercises in this book, or using any of the therapeutic methods that are mentioned herein.

The physician must be experienced in many things, but assuredly in rubbing ... for rubbing can bind a joint that is loose, and loosen a joint that is too rigid.

Hippocrates, 5th century BC

Massage

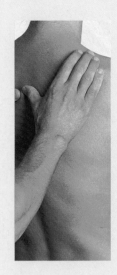

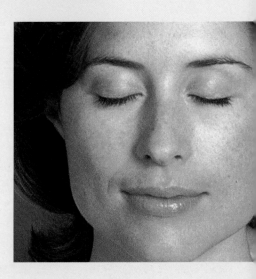

contents

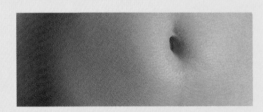

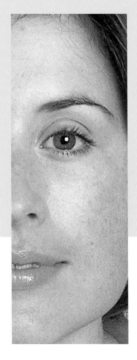

The importance of touch

In today's hectic world we are often so busy with work or education, bringing up a family and surviving financially that we don't always have time for physical contact. Yet holding out a caring hand, or hugging a friend or family member, are important elements of a healthy, happy lifestyle.

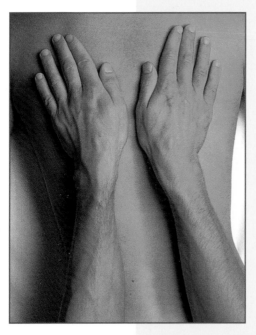

Touch is the first of the senses to develop. Our skin is covered with sensory nerve receptors that receive stimuli of heat, cold, touch, pressure and pain. Signals from touch receptors pass via sensory nerves to the spinal cord and on to the brain, where touch sensations are perceived and interpreted. This process never stops throughout life, and our bodies are always in touch 24 hours a day, even when we are asleep.

Newborn babies process most information through their skin. Inside the womb the foetus is enclosed by the walls of the uterus, which is both a comforting and a reassuring experience. After birth, the baby experiences a withdrawal of the support to which it has become accustomed over a period of nine months, so touch is vitally important to continue that feeling of support. A baby needs to be held and rocked in its mother's arms, in close contact with the warmth of her body, to help it adapt to temperature changes and open spaces in the outside world.

Touch also plays a special role as we get older and begin to feel a little less "in touch". Tactile needs do not change with ageing – if anything, they increase. Studies of long-term nursing-home residents show that those who are frequently touched demonstrate a more positive attitude about themselves. Very often an elderly person may have impaired hearing, sight or mobility, which can make them feel helpless and vulnerable. Through the emotional involvement of touch we can reach through the isolation to communicate warmth and affection. Many elderly people draw comfort from keeping a pet – not only does it provide company, but the simple act of stroking a cat or dog can provide tactile stimulation and has even been shown to lower high blood pressure.

There are huge class and cultural differences in attitudes to tactile behaviour. Some cultures are characterized by a "do not touch me" way of life, while in others there is so much embracing and kissing that it appears strange and embarrassing to non-tactile people. National and cultural differences in attitudes to touch range from the absolute non-touchability of the Japanese to the full expression of tactility found among people of countries speaking Latin-derived languages, or non-literate peoples.

Whatever our cultural background, we all have a natural ability to touch and a need to be touched. For some people this ability just needs developing – and what better way to do so than with massage? Not only is massage enjoyable for its therapeutic benefits, but it also provides a way of breaking down the barriers that sometimes separate us from each other. Massage is particularly valuable in Western society where touching is so confined and formalized. In a world full of expensive gadgets designed to make life easier, it is wonderfully satisfying to know that we can give so much pleasure simply by using our hands.

In Asia touch plays a much greater role in everyday life and healing embraces the mind, body and spirit. In the West medicine still sometimes separates physical symptoms from the person as a whole. Yet throughout history massage has been used to relieve suffering. Ancient medical records

Exchanging news and information is an extremely tactile experience for the Yanomani people who live in the Amazonian rainforest of Brazil.

describe touch as one of the physician's most valuable tools. Massage was used to promote healing long before the invention of modern drugs that freed doctors from laying hands on their patients.

Chapter One of this book describes the key massage strokes and outlines their therapeutic effects on mental and physical wellbeing. It introduces you to the properties of essential oils and shows how to blend them to create a particular aroma. Guidelines are given for preparing a massage and creating the right ambience. Experiment with the massage movements and incorporate different aromatherapy blends into your treatments for an enhanced aura of relaxation and tranquillity.

Chapter Two takes you on a voyage of discovery around the body. Each area of the body is looked at separately, with an explanation of its importance and its connection with other body-parts. The benefits of massage for each particular area are outlined in simple terms, with the various massage techniques described in stages.

Chapter Three explains how our bodies respond to the seasons. Changes in temperature and natural light can affect mood and health. Certain massage movements and particular oils can help you to accommodate these changes and enhance your sensual awareness.

Chapter Four describes the many therapeutic benefits of water, some of which you can enjoy at home. Not only do hands have amazing healing potential, but so does water – whether you are sinking into a hot bath after a long day's work, or jumping into a cool swimming pool on a hot summer's day. Many of the world's cultures recognize that you can cleanse your mind while you are purifying your body. In Ayurvedic medicine bathing is a sacred act involving massage and chanting. In Islamic countries music transforms a bath into a serene experience; in Japan bathing is traditionally an elaborate ritual that aims to calm the mind as well as deep-cleanse the body.

Chapter Five addresses the problem of stress in our modern lifestyle, caused by environmental factors, bad diet or not enough time for relaxation. Touch through massage can be one of the best ways of preventing and relieving stress. Indian head massage is particularly beneficial for mental stress, and when combined with relaxation or meditation it can work wonders. Other massage movements for stress-induced symptoms such as headaches, abdominal bloating and constipation are also outlined, together with suggestions for essential oils.

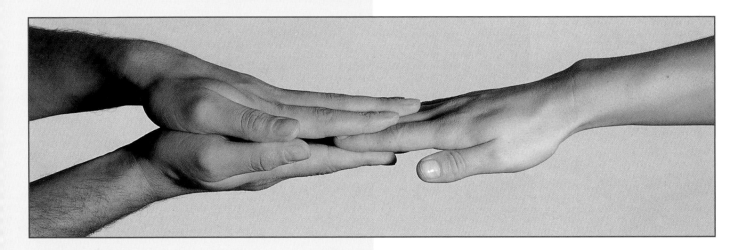

touch and fragrance

Touch is a wonderful way of breaking down the barriers that can sometimes exist between two people. Even couples who have been together for a number of years often find it difficult to touch one another without feeling self-conscious. We all have a need to be touched, and massage is the perfect way of fulfilling that need.

This chapter describes the key massage strokes and outlines their therapeutic effects on mental and physical wellbeing. When massage is coupled with the subtle powers of essential oils the senses really come into full bloom. The secrets of these oils and how to blend them are explained, together with suggestions for creating the right ambience.

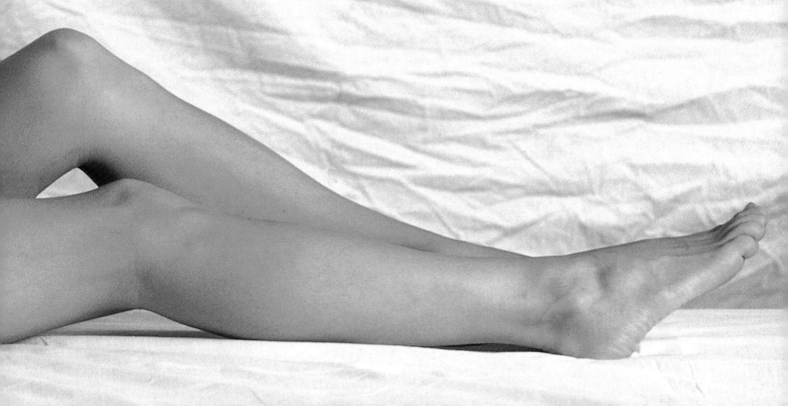

The power of massage

*[The object of massage] is to disperse the effete matters found in the muscles
and not expelled by exercise.*
Avicenna, 11th-century Arab philosopher and physician

The word massage is thought to originate from either the Greek for "knead" or the Arabic for "press safely". The people of ancient civilizations in Persia, Japan and Egypt practised the art of massage for cosmetic purposes. The Cretans oiled their bodies daily and Roman gladiators were oiled and massaged in preparation for battle. There is not much reference to massage during the Middle Ages, but in Renaissance times doctors began to incorporate it into their work. In the 19th century massage regained its popularity when Per Henrik Ling, a Swedish gymnast, combined his knowledge of gymnastics and philosophy with some old Chinese massage techniques. He introduced terms such as "effleurage" and "pettrisage".

Massage is now one of the most widely practised complementary therapies and should be thought of as a way of life rather than as a luxury. It is increasingly used alongside orthodox medicine for treating a range of ailments, many of which are attributed to stress and tension. When repressed emotions, which often manifest themselves in the muscles, are released through massage both mind and body benefit. Massage need not be time-consuming: just a 10- or 15-minute back massage can be therapeutic because the spine is the centre of all the body's functions – 33 pairs of nerves fan out from the spinal cord. A foot or hand massage is also particularly beneficial because all the reflexology points (pressure points that are linked to various parts of the body by nerves) are stimulated.

There are many different types of massage: some techniques work on pressure points, while others work on specific areas to eliminate toxins. Massage can stimulate the lymphatic system, break down stubborn fat, or work at a deeper level to promote the body's natural healing ability. The numerous benefits include improved circulation, digestion and skin condition.

Secrets of essential oils

Touch is one of our primary senses and, when combined with the sense of smell (as in an aromatherapy massage), provides the ultimate feel-good therapy. We are surrounded by thousands of different scents, but many of us are unaware of the power of smell and its effect on the mind and emotions. The olfactory nerves in the brain, which are stimulated by smelling, are in direct contact with the limbic system. The olfactory area is connected to the hypothalamus, which has an important influence on the pituitary gland that controls the hormonal system. This explains why odors can stimulate memories, recreate experiences, warn us of danger, arouse or comfort us.

The practice of aromatherapy dates back thousands of years to Egypt, China and Greece. The Egyptians used essential oils cosmetically and therapeutically, and certain oils were used for embalming the dead. Wealthy Chinese households burned the mugwort plant during childbirth because they believed it helped labor and soothed a newborn baby. Hippocrates claimed that the secret of good health was to have an aromatic bath and a scented massage every day.

In about AD 1000 Avicenna, the great Arab physician, discovered the aromatic properties of the rose and perfected the process of distillation in order to capture a plant's true essence. By the 13th century lavender was being grown in England; its benefits were rediscovered accidentally by the French chemist René Maurice Gattefosse in the 1920s. When he burned his hand in the laboratory, he accidentally plunged the affected part into a bowl of lavender oil instead of water. He was amazed by how quickly the pain disappeared and how fast the scar healed, and this led him to carry out further research on other essential oils, provoking a wave of interest throughout Europe. Oils such as clove, thyme and lemon were already being used to sterilize medical instruments and fumigate hospital wards, and now it was found that they had an effect on a wide range of complaints: they could stimulate the immune system, help skin conditions, improve digestive problems, relieve anxiety and depression, and treat open wounds. Dr Jean Valnet, who succeeded Gattefosse, used essential oils in the treament of wounds during World War II and in 1980 he wrote *The Practice of Aromatherapy*.

Marguerite Maury, an Austrian biochemist and beauty therapist, was inspired by Gattefosse's work. She devised a special massage using essential oils and concocted several blends for her clients' individual ailments, which ranged from skin problems, insomnia, and aches and pains, to just feeling emotionally under the weather. Maury won two international prizes for her research. It is through the work of people like Gattefosse, Valnet and Maury that aromatherapy is as popular and accessible as it is today.

Blending essential oils

Essential oils are often referred to as the "soul" of a plant. They are produced by tiny glands in the petals of flowers, in the wood, stems and barks of trees, and in the skins of many fruits. Each oil is composed of at least 100 different chemical constituents, which are categorized as aldehydes, oxides, ketones, phenols, esters, terpenes and alcohols. Oils have individual characteristics and when blended the different chemicals together produce a specific property – such as relaxing, uplifting or sedative – and a distinct aroma. About 300 oils are known for their healing powers, and more are continually being discovered. However, not all are used in aromatherapy.

The principal reasons for blending essential oils are to incorporate their different healing properties and create a particular aroma. There are no strict rules about blending, which is why aromatherapy can be a wonderful path of discovery. Before using a particular blend I always allow the person being massaged to smell it first, to make sure that they like it, for an aroma can smell completely different to individual noses and on different types of skin. Everyone has their unique body odor, which is governed by a wide range of factors such as genetic history, race, state of health, hormonal changes, and the effects of medication or pregnancy. This explains why a certain perfume may smell entirely different on two different people.

There is also an aromatic "orchestra" to consider when blending essential oils. The 19th-century perfumier Septimus Piesse devised an odor scale based on the musical scale, with oils falling into three groups according to their rate of evaporation – these are the top, middle and base notes. Top notes, such as tea tree, eucalyptus, mandarin, lemon, orange, bergamot, basil and coriander, have a light quality and form a scent's first impression because of their fast evaporation rate. These oils are mostly stimulants, and their aroma does not last long. The middle scale notes, such as geranium, lavender, marjoram, rosewood, rosemary, fennel, rose otto and ylang- ylang, are the heart of a fragrance. These oils have a medium

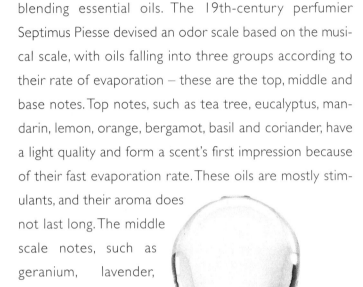

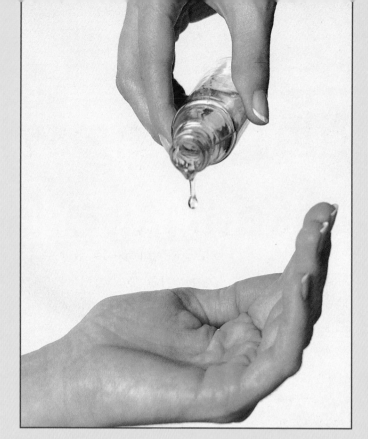

rate of evaporation and their scent is not always apparent on first impression. Middle-note oils last a little longer than the top notes and are generally good for the whole body. The base notes, such as rose, jasmine, benzoin, frankincense, myrrh, patchouli, vetiver and sandalwood, evaporate slowly. These heavier scents are slower to surface but linger longer. They have a strong influence on the overall blend by "fixing" the other essences. Base note oils have sedative properties.

Creating essential oil blends is similar to composing a musical score – you need the correct balance of sounds. You have to "listen" through the nose and remember that a blend doesn't just happen, it develops. Once you become familiar with nature's aromatic orchestra you can trust your intuition to create your own scented symphony. Remember to use only small amounts of the strong-scented oils and more of the lighter-scented oils.

When used for massage, essential oils must always be diluted in a base, or carrier, oil. Sweet almond and cold-pressed sunflower oils are both popular because they are light, or you can use any good-quality wheatgerm, jojoba, evening primrose, avocado, hazelnut or peach kernel oil. For a face massage you will need one drop of essential oil in 2ml of carrier oil. For a whole body massage add two to six drops of essential oil to 10ml of carrier oil. For sensitive skins use a more dilute mixture.

Oils should always be stored in a cool dark place in dark glass bottles, and the caps should be tight to prevent oxidation. Nowadays you can buy very attractive boxes for storing essential oils. It is better to make up blends in small amounts to avoid them becoming rancid. If you are making a larger blend, add a small amount of wheatgerm oil – this is a good stabilizer and will prolong the oil's life if it is kept in the refrigerator.

The fragrance families

Essential oil fragrances fall into one of five families. Studies have shown that woody or spicy oils usually appeal more to men, floral and citrus to women. The green family of oils have a general appeal to both sexes. Aromas from the same oil family tend to blend well together.

- **Citrus:** *bergamot, grapefruit, lemon, mandarin, orange*
- **Floral:** *camomile, geranium, jasmine, lavender, melissa, neroli, rose, ylang-ylang*
- **Green:** *basil, eucalyptus, peppermint, rosemary, sweet marjoram*
- **Spicy:** *black pepper, juniper berry, myrrh, tea tree*
- **Woody:** *cedarwood, cypress, frankincense, pine, rosewood, sandalwood*

Essential oils are often divided into mood-enhancing groups.

- **Stimulating:** *basil, black pepper, coriander, eucalyptus, lemon, lemon-grass, peppermint, pine, sage, rosemary, thyme*
- **Refreshing:** *basil, bergamot, cypress, geranium, juniper, lavender, lemon, lemon-grass, lime, mandarin, melissa, orange, peppermint, petitgrain, rosemary, pine*
- **Warming:** *benzoin, black pepper, cajeput, camomile, clary sage, clove, coriander, ginger, marjoram*
- **Relaxing:** *benzoin, camomile, cedarwood, clary sage, frankincense, geranium, jasmine, lavender, marjoram, neroli, patchouli, petitgrain, rose, rosewood, sandalwood, ylang-ylang*

Massaging with essential oils

The main purpose of massage is to balance the body's subtle energies. If the flow of these energies becomes obstructed, both physical and emotional disharmony can occur. When massage is combined with aromatherapy, the scents of the essential oils can themselves assist in relaxation, helping to rebalance the emotional tension that often leads to muscle tension.

An aromatherapy massage is performed more slowly and lightly than traditional massage. It can take anything from a few minutes to a couple of hours for the oils to be absorbed into the body, depending on a person's state of health and the amount of fatty tissue.

Aromatherapy massage can be beneficial during pregnancy, but avoid the abdomen until after the fifth month. To prevent stretchmarks an expectant mother should massage wheatgerm or sweet almond oil with a 2–3 percent dilution of neroli or mandarin oil lightly over the abdominal and hip area. Geranium oil is good for swollen ankles.

Babies can also benefit from an aromatherapy massage, using a low dilution (one drop in 10ml). Camomile or lavender oil massaged gently in a clockwise direction on the baby's abdomen or lower back is particularly beneficial for colic pain. Both oils are also soothing for diaper rash. Mandarin can be used for constipation. Not only will massage provide a natural means of bonding with a baby, it will also be comforting and encourage sleep.

Cautions and contra-indications

- Do not take essential oils internally.
- Do not apply oils directly to the skin, with the exception of lavender and tea tree in moderation.
- Keep oils away from the eyes: if an accident occurs, wash the eyes with water.
- Avoid aromatherapy massage after a heavy meal.
- Do not massage over skin infections or septic areas, thrombosis or phlebitis.
- If you are allergic to certain perfumes, make sure that none of the ingredients of a blended oil will cause a reaction.
- If taking homeopathic medicine it is advisable to avoid using black pepper, camphor, eucalyptus, and peppermint. .

- If sunbathing or using a sunbed, avoid using bergamot, lemon, orange and verbena as they can react under ultraviolet light.
- Epileptics should avoid hyssop, sweet fennel and wormwood.
- Hypertensives (sufferers from high blood pressure) should avoid hyssop, rosehip, sage and thyme.
- Anyone suffering from cancer should check with their doctor before using essential oils.
- Essential oils should be avoided during chemotherapy or in conjunction with certain medication.
- Oils of arnica, basil, birch, cedarwood, clary sage, cypress, fennel, juniper, marjoram, peppermint, rosemary, sage and thyme should never be used during pregnancy.

Preparing a massage

Massage should be a relaxing experience for both giver and receiver, and it is extremely important to create the right atmosphere. If possible, use a room that has a soft, subtle décor: pale pink, peach and cream make relaxing background colours, whereas blue can often look cold. The room should be warm (72°F/22°C) because body temperature drops during massage and if the muscles get cold they will contract, thus counteracting the benefits of the treatment. Keep any areas of the body that are not being massaged covered with towels.

The lighting should be soft: if you have dimmer switches these are ideal for controlling the effects of harsh lighting on the eyes. Candles placed in a safe area give a wonderful warm light – you can add a couple of drops of essential oil to the melted wax at the top of a candle to create an aroma, or you may like to use an essence burner. Make sure that the oil you are burning is compatible with the blend you are using for the massage. If possible ensure a noise-free zone by switching off telephones and answerphones and playing some light relaxing music to counteract traffic noise. Gentle music will help both partners to relax into the rhythm of the massage movements and also to become aware of breathing slowly and deeply.

Ideally massage should be carried out on a purpose-built couch, but in the home you can improvise with a duvet, a futon or a length of foam. Using a bed often puts a strain on the back of the masseur, especially if the mattress is not firm. Whichever you choose, be sure to cover it well with towels to protect it from the oil. When your partner is lying on their front a bolster or rolled-up towel should be placed under the ankles to take any pressure off the knees. It is also advisable to place a pillow under a man's pelvis. When your partner is lying on their back, support their head with a small flat cushion, use a pillow under the lower back area if there are any back problems, and use the bolster or rolled-up towel under the knees. If your partner wears contact lenses it is best to remove them, and long hair should be tied away from the face.

A masseur's hands should be clean and the nails should be kept short. Always apply essential oil to your own hands to warm it before starting any massage movement. Never pour oil directly from the bottle on to your partner's body. Use just enough oil to be able to slide your hands without slipping over the area to be massaged. When you need to apply more oil, try not to break the physical contact – always leave one hand on your partner's body to maintain the continuity of touch.

Effleurage

The term effleurage comes from the French word *effleurer*, meaning "to skim over" or "to stroke". It is an ideal movement for opening a massage session, because the rhythmic strokes allow the recipient to become acquainted with the therapist's hands. Effleurage is very comforting: it is a wonderful way of warming the area to be worked and a good means of applying oil to the body. It should be performed slowly and rhythmically.

Effleurage can be used on all areas of the body, although the hands may be used in different ways for different parts. Flat-hand effleurage is used on the back, which is the largest flat area. Using the flat of the hand, long strokes are made in the direction that the blood flows to the heart and the lymph towards the lymph nodes (see page 88). The main pressure is on the upward stroke, with lighter pressure on the downward stroke. This technique can also be used on both the fronts and the backs of the legs — although, depending on the size of the legs, cupped-hand effleurage is also sometimes used, particularly on the calves. For smaller, more delicate areas of the body, just the fingertips are used. The hands may be used alternately, or both together, or one hand may support the other during a movement. The strokes should follow the natural contours of the body.

Effleurage can be deep or superficial. Deep effleurage stimulates the capillary circulation in the skin and improves the skin's elasticity as the sebaceous glands secrete more sebum to create a softer, more supple texture. It can be interspersed with all the other massage movements, providing continuity throughout a treatment.

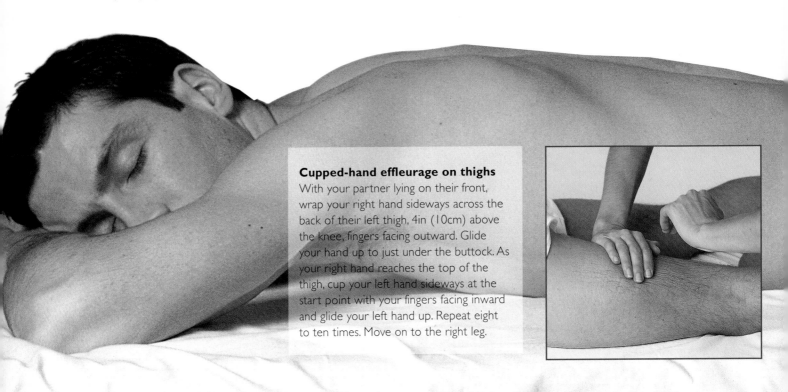

Cupped-hand effleurage on thighs
With your partner lying on their front, wrap your right hand sideways across the back of their left thigh, 4in (10cm) above the knee, fingers facing outward. Glide your hand up to just under the buttock. As your right hand reaches the top of the thigh, cup your left hand sideways at the start point with your fingers facing inward and glide your left hand up. Repeat eight to ten times. Move on to the right leg.

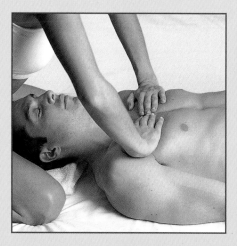

Upper chest and shoulders

1 Kneel astride your partner's head. Once you have applied oil to your hands, gently place them on the middle of the upper chest with your fingers pointing in toward each other. The pressure should not be too firm because the chest is a sensitive area. Once you have made contact for a few seconds, slowly glide both hands out toward the shoulders.

2 Continue to effleurage by turning your fingers outward, while at the same time moving your hands around the shoulders. Gently push the shoulders down using the heels of your hands. It often helps to lean slightly forward as you press down, but be careful not to strain your own back.

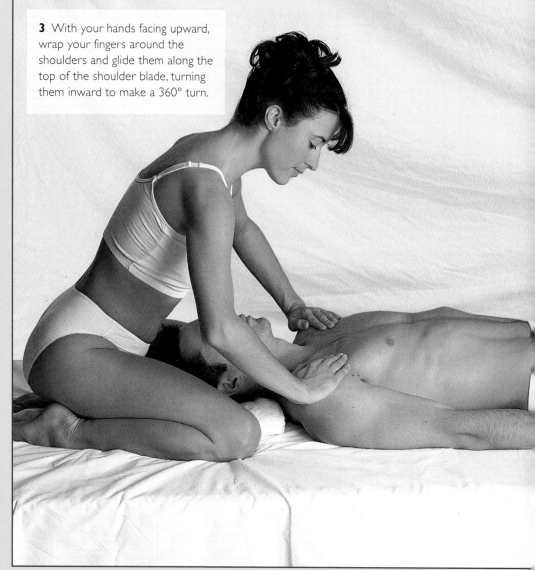

3 With your hands facing upward, wrap your fingers around the shoulders and glide them along the top of the shoulder blade, turning them inward to make a 360° turn.

4 (right) When your fingers have met at the base of the neck, gradually allow one hand to slip on top of the other. Be careful not to place your thumbs on the throat area – they must be kept at the sides or back of the neck. Gently draw your hands up to the base of the skull, giving the neck a little stretch at the same time. Release your hands gently and repeat the whole movement two to four times, drawing your hands up the back of the head as you do it for the final time.

Petrissage

Petrissage comes from the French word *pétrir*, meaning "to knead". It is the term used for any stroke that presses down the tissues to break up areas of muscular tension, and includes kneading, wringing and skin rolling. It is normally applied with the balls of the thumbs or fingers to soft tissue areas over bone, or to individual muscles, and is particularly beneficial on the neck, shoulders, buttocks and legs – all areas where tension accumulates. The rhythmic lifting and squeezing action pumps nutrients through the muscles and tissues, and the pressure on the deeper blood and lymph vessels encourages accumulated waste products to be eliminated.

This moderate-to-deep stroke is usually worked in a circular or transverse direction that allows the masseur to locate particular areas of muscle tightness. It is best not to concentrate on a tight area for too long, but rather to work on it for a while and then return again a little later, if necessary.

You can use one hand to perform the movement while resting the other, or both hands together to squeeze the muscle in opposite directions. As with all massage movements, keep your hands as relaxed as possible and try not to tense your own body. Allow your body weight to carry you into each movement.

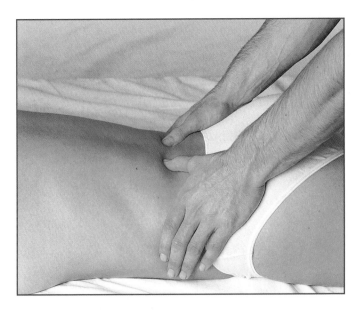

Petrissage using thumbs

1 Kneel astride your partner's legs, or to one side (although this may mean slightly twisting your own back in order to carry out the movement). Place the pads of your thumbs downward on either side of the spine at the sacral area. Press down and slightly forward with your thumbs and then gently release.

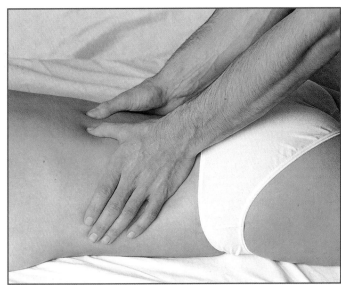

2 Continue this movement, gradually working all the way up the spine. You will have to raise your body off your heels as you move further up the back. You may notice a little redness each time you press on the skin – this is a good sign that blood circulation is increasing in that area, which will help the muscles to loosen. Repeat two or three times.

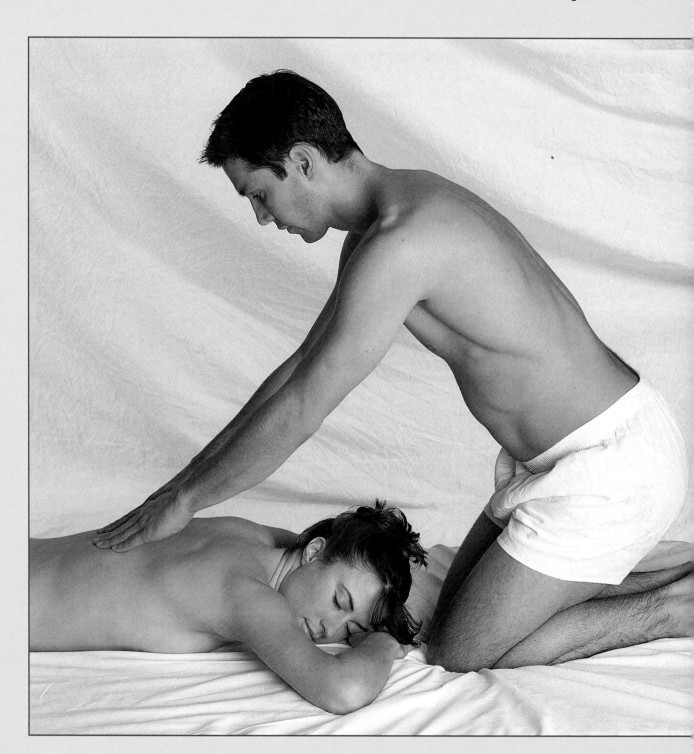

Petrissage using fingertips

Kneel at your partner's head and place your hands, fingers together and palms down, at the top of their back on either side of the spine. Gently push down and forward with your fingertips, and then release the pressure a little. Continue this movement all the way down the spine. Repeat two or three times.

Kneading

Kneading is the most popular petrissage movement and without it no therapeutic massage would be complete. It should only be used after the muscles have been prepared and warmed with strokes such as effleurage. There are many variations, depending on the area being treated, but basically the thumb and fingers are used as if kneading dough, alternately squeezing and releasing the flesh. This relaxes the muscles and drains away any toxins, and is also beneficial for breaking down fat and improving the metabolism and blood supply. Kneading is a very versatile movement: when performed slowly it promotes relaxation, but when done vigorously it can be invigorating – the more vigorous the movement, the more you will stimulate the circulation and energize the body.

Kneading works particularly well on fleshy areas such as the hips, thighs and buttocks where excess fluid and fat can accumulate. It is also wonderful for tension in the neck, shoulders and calves. Avoid any areas where there are broken capillaries or varicose veins. As with any massage strokes, the firmer the pressure the more you will address the deeper underlying muscles, whereas a lighter pressure will affect the superficial layer of muscles. It is important not to pinch the flesh when kneading. It is easier to grasp and squeeze the flesh by using the whole of your hand – if you do use just the fingers you may find yourself pinching the flesh instead of kneading it. For a sluggish digestive system, light kneading is effective on the abdominal area (unless it is distended or painful). Be cautious on areas of skin that are extremely hairy, where the kneading action could be uncomfortable.

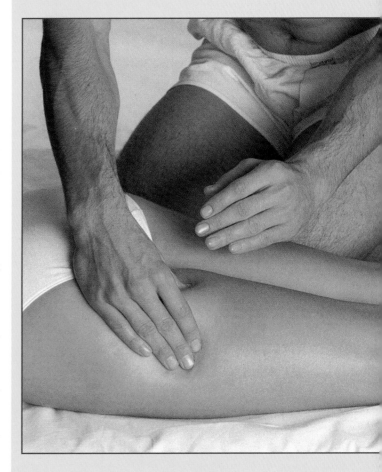

Kneading the thighs

1 Place a small pillow under your partner's abdomen to support the lower back and pelvic area. Oil the back of the thigh with a few effleurage strokes. Sit on the opposite side of the leg to be worked on and place your hands over the muscles at the back of the thigh. Press your right hand into the muscle and squeeze the muscle between your thumb and fingers.

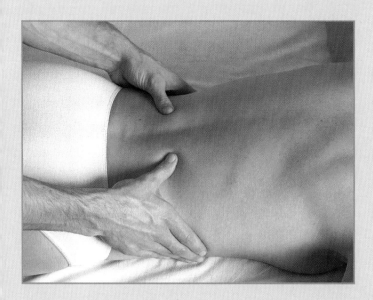

Thumb circling

Support your partner's lower back with a small pillow, if necessary. Sit to one side or kneel astride your partner's legs. Place your thumbs on either side of the spine just below the waistline and rotate them away from each other in small circular movements. Keep your thumbs straight but not rigid, being careful not to bend or flex them because this will put pressure on the joints. Continue to circle your thumbs all over the lower back and sacral area to disperse any toxins and release muscular tension.

Feathering

(right) This is a wonderfully relaxing way of finishing the sequence of massage movements on the back. Stroke very lightly down the back with your fingertips, using both hands together or one hand at a time. As one hand approaches the lower back, the other hand begins the movement between the shoulders – you should not lose contact with the body at all. This movement calms the energy that has been generated during all the other movements.

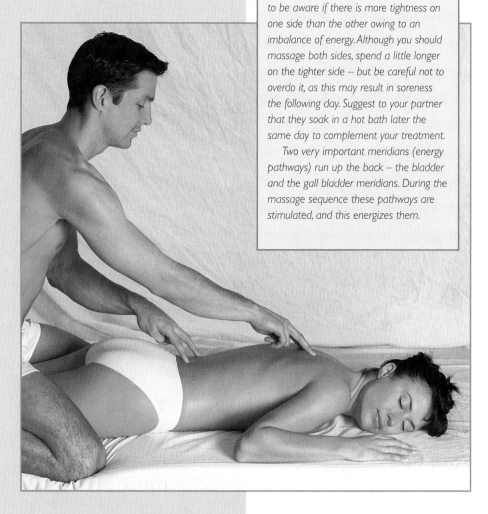

It is important when massaging the back to be aware if there is more tightness on one side than the other owing to an imbalance of energy. Although you should massage both sides, spend a little longer on the tighter side – but be careful not to overdo it, as this may result in soreness the following day. Suggest to your partner that they soak in a hot bath later the same day to complement your treatment.

Two very important meridians (energy pathways) run up the back – the bladder and the gall bladder meridians. During the massage sequence these pathways are stimulated, and this energizes them.

The neck and shoulders

The neck and shoulders are the main areas prone to tension in your body. The neck is very delicate and yet it has to support the head, which is a heavy part of the body, weighing approximately 14lb (6kg). Like the back, the neck and shoulder muscles help you to perform daily activities such as carrying shopping, driving, gardening, doing domestic chores, lifting babies, pushing buggies, even using a knife and fork.

Many emotional feelings are carried in the neck and shoulder area – we literally carry our burdens on our shoulders. Bad posture, such as hunching your shoulders when you feel cold or nervous, also affects this area. This causes the muscles at the sides and back of the neck to become very tense. When the neck muscles become imbalanced, headaches can occur. If the shoulder muscles are tense, the range of movement in the shoulder, arm and neck can be affected. Some sports, such as golf, soft-ball, tennis, swimming and bowling, can also create neck and shoulder problems – so it is important that this area of the body is kept free of tension and discomfort. Shoulder massage can also stimulate the gall bladder and liver, because the related meridians pass through this area.

Petrissage

1 Turn your partner's head to the left and sit or stand on their right. Bend their right arm gently round so that the hand rests across the lower back. This stroke should not be carried out on anyone with long-term shoulder or arm problems. Support and slightly elevate the right shoulder joint with your right hand, and use the edge of your left hand to massage around the shoulder blade.

2 Continue to slide the edge of your hand all the way down and around the shoulder blade. At the same time, keep the shoulder joint elevated with your right hand. This loosens the shoulder, allowing you to massage right underneath the area. Repeat two to five times and then work on the other shoulder blade. This is a good movement for freeing tension and stiffness, and for releasing muscle tightness.

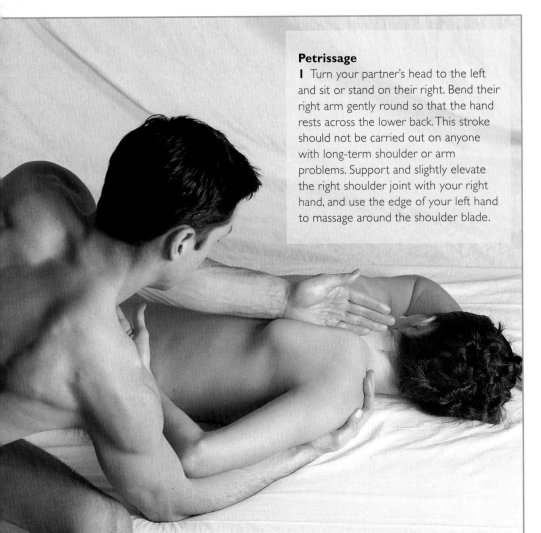

Kneading

Turn your partner's head to the left. Place your hands across the top of the right shoulder. Starting with your right hand, squeeze the shoulder muscle between your thumb and fingers, then repeat with your left hand. Working rhythmically, continue to knead the tension from the muscle using both hands alternately, gradually moving along the whole shoulder muscle. Repeat on the other shoulder, with your partner's head turned to the right.

Thumb circling

Turn your partner's head to one side with their shoulders as relaxed as possible. Place your thumbs between the tops of the shoulder blades on either side of the spine and slowly rotate them in small outward circles, working down the spine a little and further out toward the shoulders. This movement is extremely versatile because it can also be carried out while someone is sitting and even through clothes (without the use of oil, of course).

Effleurage

1 Your partner's forehead should be resting on their hands with their shoulders as relaxed as possible. Stand or sit to the side of your partner's head, and place your right hand across the base of the neck so that your fingers wrap around one side of the neck and your thumb curls round the other side. Squeezing gently, slowly scoop your right hand from the base of the neck to the top, finishing level with the base of the skull, as shown.

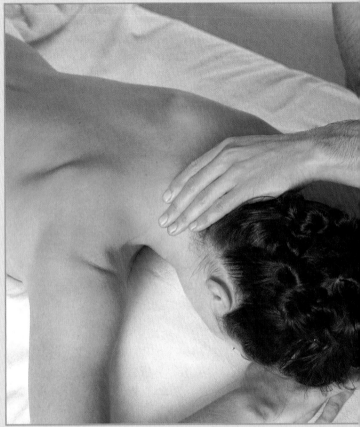

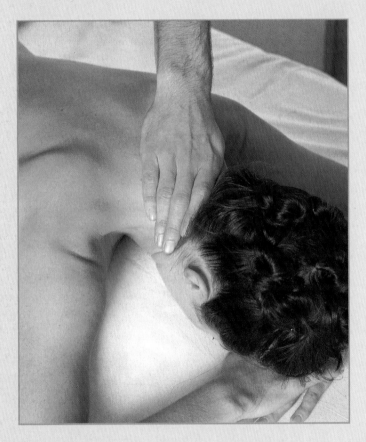

2 Now, place your left hand at the top of the neck in line with the base of the skull, positioning the thumb and fingers in the same way as before. Squeezing your thumb gently toward your fingers, draw your hand downward toward the bottom of the neck. Continue stages 1 and 2, using first the right hand then the left, alternately moving upward and downward. This will relieve muscle tension and slightly stretch the neck at the same time.

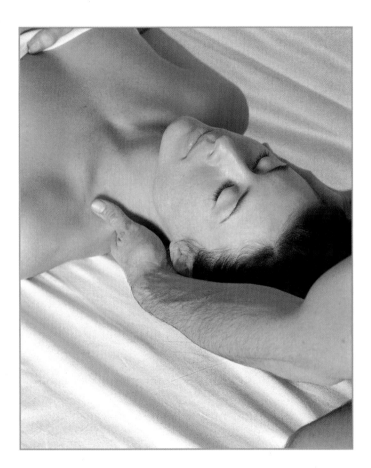

2 (below) Slowly draw your left hand up the neck until it reaches the base of the skull. As your left hand becomes level with the base of the skull, place your right hand under the bottom of the neck, positioning the fingers in the same way. Slowly draw this hand upward along the neck. The action is a gentle stroking movement using both hands alternately to pull upward along the neck, giving it a little bit of a stretch at the same time. Repeat the movement eight to ten times, keeping it smooth and gentle.

Stroking

1 (above) Ask your partner to lie on their back (do not use a pillow to support your partner's head because it needs to be completely free). Place your left hand under their neck so that your fingers are underneath and your thumb is relaxed along the side of the neck. Be careful not to place your thumb across the throat area.

The buttocks

Many people are uncomfortable with the thought of a buttock massage. If you are at ease with your partner, ask them whether they would like this area massaged. It is better to give them the option rather than to go ahead assuming it will be acceptable, which could lead to feelings of embarrassment or anxiety.

A buttock massage can be enormously beneficial because so much tension is stored there. This is an area of our anatomy that we tend to disregard, but it is not just a means of sitting. All the gluteal (buttock) muscles are constantly active, helping us to stand up, walk, climb stairs and drive cars. Dancers and sportspeople, such as footballers, ice skaters, cyclists and jockeys, build up a large amount of tension in the buttocks and therefore need regular massage in this area. Anyone with lower back and hip problems can also benefit from massage because once the gluteal muscles are relaxed and the tension is released there will be less tightness in the adjoining areas. Cellulite, fluid retention and excess fat can all be reduced by using the techniques that follow.

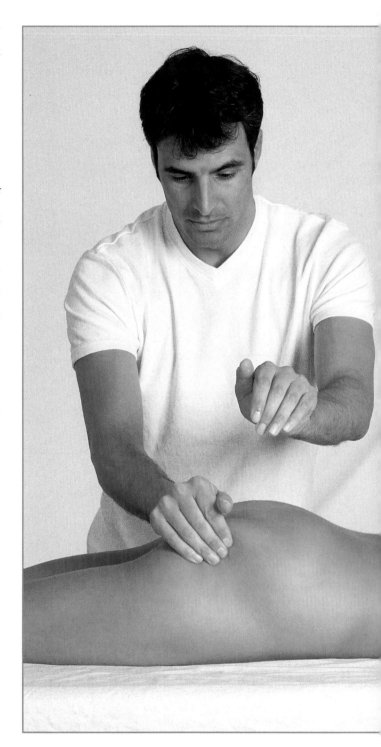

Cupping
Stand or sit to one side of your partner. Reaching across their body, place your hands on the buttock in a cupped position with fingers together but not too rigid. The action should be light and quick as you lift one hand up while lowering the other. Keeping the hands well cupped and the arms as relaxed as possible, repeat the movement continuously all over the buttock area. Move to the other side if you wish before repeating the movement on the other buttock.

Hacking

Stand or sit to one side of your partner in line with their hips. Using the edges of your hands, but keeping the fingers relaxed and close together, bring down first your left hand and then the right to hit the buttock. Keep your hands close to the buttock as you continue the movement, maintaining an even rhythm. Once you have mastered the technique of hacking you will be able to increase the speed. Work all over the buttock, and alternate with cupping for a really stimulating effect. Repeat the hacking on the other buttock.

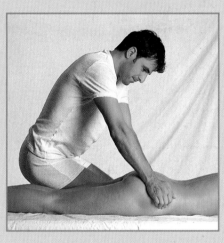

Petrissage

1 Sit or kneel to one side of your partner, facing their head. Place the heels of both hands on top of each buttock so that your fingers are pointing out toward the hips. Push down with the heels of your hands and gradually slide them outward, squeezing each buttock between the heel of your hand and your fingers.

2 Continue to slide out and down toward the hip area. Repeat the whole movement from the top of the buttock out to the side of the hip four to six times.

The backs of the legs

When we are standing our legs bear the whole weight of our bodies. The bones in our legs are the largest in the body and they are supported by a range of muscle groups. The backs of the legs tend to be neglected simply because we are unable to see or touch them easily, so everyone can benefit from massage in this area. By stimulating the circulation of the blood, massage can increase the supply of nutrients to the legs. Active people, such as athletes and dancers, can benefit from massage on the backs of the legs, either before exercise to warm up the muscles, or afterward to loosen tight muscles and eliminate fatigue.

Cellulite and fluid retention, both of which occur at the tops of the thighs, respond well to massage. Fluid retention is also very common around the ankles, especially during pregnancy. Be careful when massaging the backs of the legs not to put too much pressure on the area at the back of the knees, as this could affect the joint. Cupped-hand effleurage should only be carried out when the area has been warmed.

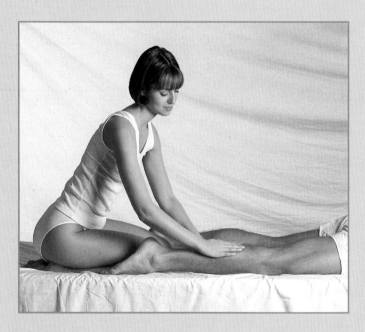

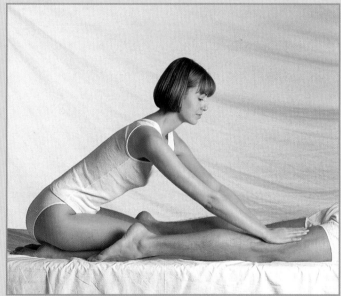

Effleurage

1 Kneel by your partner's feet and place your oiled hands just above the ankle on the leg to be masssaged, with your palms and fingers facing downward. Hold your hands there for a few moments to make contact before starting the movement. Slowly glide your hands up the lower leg, feeling the contours of the calf muscle. Continue over the back of the knee, but at this stage ease the pressure slightly so that no strain is placed on the knee joint.

2 Once your hands have passed over the knee area apply a little more pressure as you continue to effleurage up the thigh. At this stage you may have to sit up off your heels to reach the upper thigh. Be careful not to take any of the strain in your back. Once your hands have reached the top of the thigh just under the buttock, turn them in slightly toward each other before moving on to stage 3.

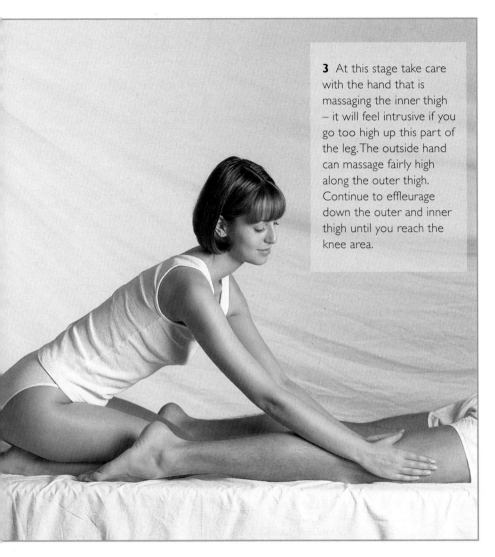

3 At this stage take care with the hand that is massaging the inner thigh – it will feel intrusive if you go too high up this part of the leg. The outside hand can massage fairly high along the outer thigh. Continue to effleurage down the outer and inner thigh until you reach the knee area.

4 (above) Slowly draw your hands down the sides of the calf muscle, slightly squeezing it between your hands at the same time. Finally, finish with your hands in the starting position, ready to repeat all four stages once or twice more before moving to the other leg.

When carrying out any effleurage movements it is beneficial to really "breathe" into the stroke. Take a deep breath in to prepare yourself, then breathe out as you effleurage up the body and in as you effleurage down the body. Encourage your partner to breathe in the same manner during this stroke.

Cupped-hand effleurage

1 (right) Sit to the side of the leg you are about to massage and place your left hand in a cupped position on your partner's lower leg about 3–4in (7–10cm) above the ankle. Your arms should be slightly bent from the elbow and not held too rigid. Slowly glide your hand over the calf muscle up to the area just under the knee. As your left hand approaches the top, start the same movement with your right hand.

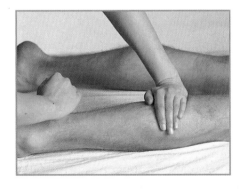

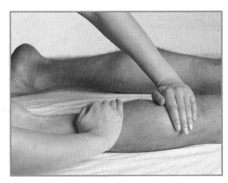

2 (above) Keeping your hands cupped all the time, with your fingers facing the inner or outer leg, continue the stroke slowly but rhythmically, using alternate hands and leaning slightly into the movement.

Thumb glides

1 Sit either to one side of your partner or at their feet. Place the pads of both your thumbs just above the right ankle on either side of the Achilles tendon. Be careful not to put any pressure on the tendon. Slowly glide your thumbs alongside the tendon and continue over the calf muscle until you reach the area just below the knee. Use your intuition to decide how deep the pressure should be – the lower leg can be very sensitive in some people.

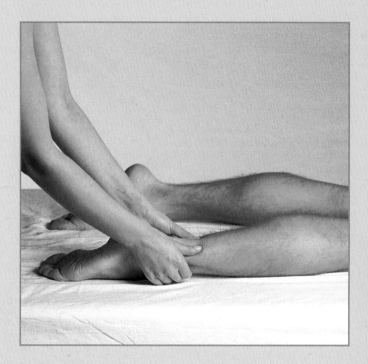
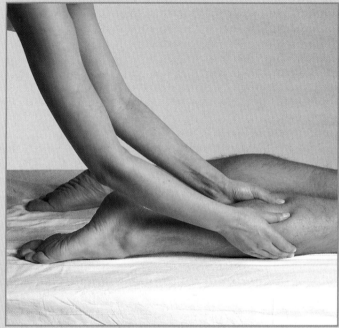

2 Once you have reached the area just below the knee, relieve the thumb pressure and curl your fingers round so that they are cradling the calf. Slowly glide them down the outer leg to the ankle, then place your thumbs in the starting position ready to repeat the movement. The thumbs glide up the lower leg but the fingers stroke back down the leg. Repeat two to three times before changing to the other leg.

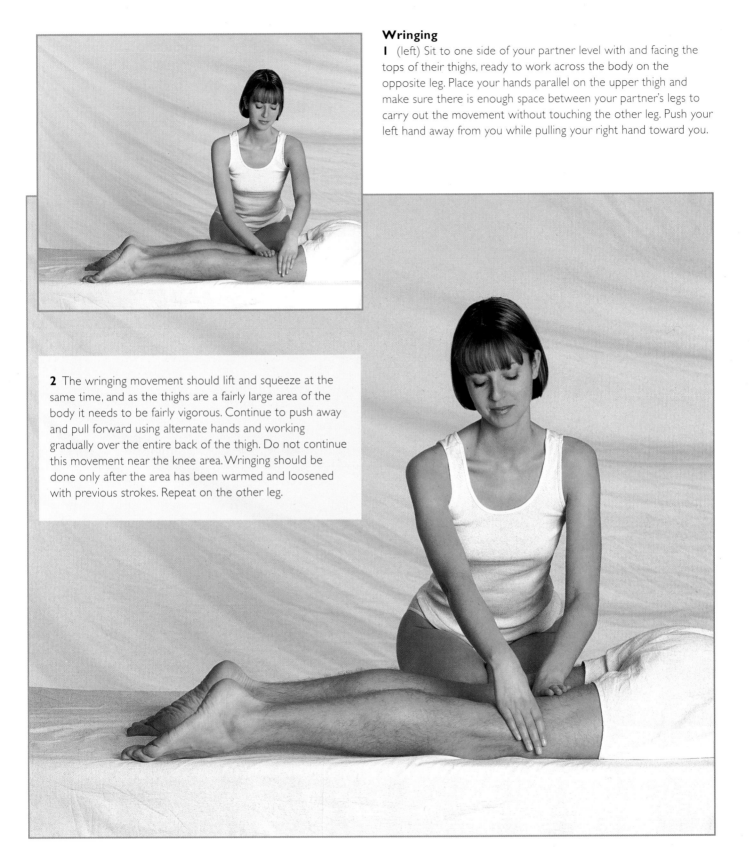

Wringing

1 (left) Sit to one side of your partner level with and facing the tops of their thighs, ready to work across the body on the opposite leg. Place your hands parallel on the upper thigh and make sure there is enough space between your partner's legs to carry out the movement without touching the other leg. Push your left hand away from you while pulling your right hand toward you.

2 The wringing movement should lift and squeeze at the same time, and as the thighs are a fairly large area of the body it needs to be fairly vigorous. Continue to push away and pull forward using alternate hands and working gradually over the entire back of the thigh. Do not continue this movement near the knee area. Wringing should be done only after the area has been warmed and loosened with previous strokes. Repeat on the other leg.

The face

The muscles in the face are the smallest in the body and, unlike larger body muscles, they do not attach bone to bone (with the exception of the jaw). The facial muscles attach the facial bones to the skin, and the areas of skin to other parts of the face. They cq-ordinate our many facial expressions, such as smiling, frowning, chewing and crying, so it is no wonder that they become tense and tired. Even when we are sleeping the facial muscles are rarely completely relaxed.

A facial massage can be a treatment in itself, or be incorporated in a body massage. Until you experience a massage on your face, you will probably be unaware of just how much tension your facial muscles hold. Massage movements on the face are small and delicate so they are usually performed with the fingertips. This allows the masseur to feel the contours of the face. A masseur's nails must always be kept short.

Facial massage is marvellous for the skin: it increases the circulation and lymph flow, or relaxes tired, taut muscles; it relieves headaches and eyestrain, and generally rejuvenates and refreshes the appearance of the face. All in all, it is far cheaper and more relaxing than a face-lift!

Thumb glides

1 Support your partner's head with a small flat cushion or a folded towel. Unless your partner has exceptionally dry skin, use only a little oil for the massage. Sit or kneel behind your partner's head and place the pads of your thumbs just above the eyebrows in the centre of the forehead. Your fingers should be relaxed and cradling the head, and your thumbs parallel with the heels of your hands. Start to glide both thumbs outward.

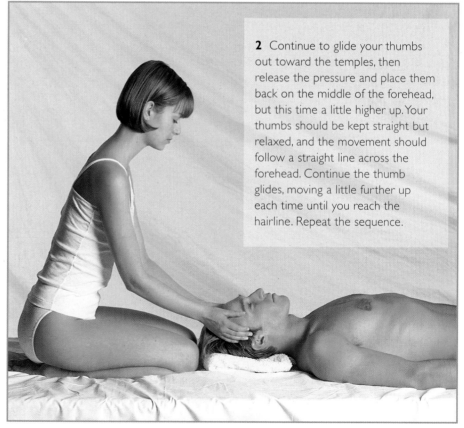

2 Continue to glide your thumbs out toward the temples, then release the pressure and place them back on the middle of the forehead, but this time a little higher up. Your thumbs should be kept straight but relaxed, and the movement should follow a straight line across the forehead. Continue the thumb glides, moving a little further up each time until you reach the hairline. Repeat the sequence.

Thumb glides

(left) If your partner is wearing contact lenses they should be removed before working anywhere near the eyes. Ask your partner to close their eyes. Place your thumbs gently on either side of the top of the nose, allowing your fingers to rest on the sides of the face. Glide your thumbs outward toward the cheekbones, being careful not to drag the skin. Once your thumbs have reached the cheekbones, release them and bring them back to the same starting point. Repeat the movement a few times. Massaging this area is useful for dispersing congestion caused by sinus problems.

Thumb circles

(right) Kneel just behind your partner's head. Gently place your hands so that the pads of your thumbs are resting on the temples and your fingers are cradling the head just behind the ears. Press your thumbs gently into the temples and slowly rotate them in a continuous movement. Ask your partner if the pressure is too deep, and if not increase it a little. After you have done a series of circles hold your thumbs still on the temples for a few seconds before removing them gradually.

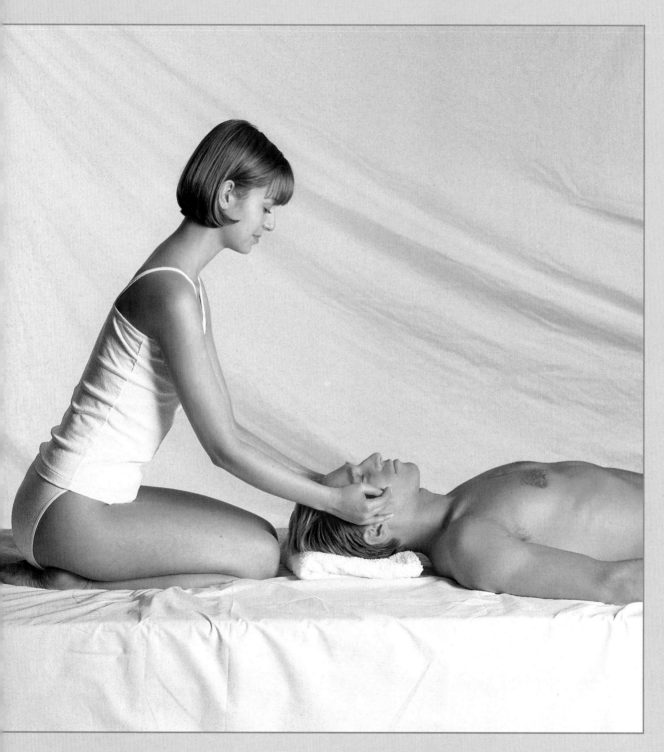

Stroking under the cheekbones
Ask your partner to close their eyes. Place your hands under their cheekbone about ½in (1cm) away from their nose. Keeping your fingers relaxed, use the edge of your little finger together with the tip of your third finger to slowly stroke under the bone outward toward the ear. Release your hands and bring them back to the starting point to repeat the movement. Really feel the contour of the cheekbone as you carry out this movement and don't be afraid to put a little pressure into it. Repeat two to four times.

Stroking around the jaw

1 Your partner should have their eyes closed. Gently place your hands with your fingertips on the middle of the chin so that you have either side of the jawbone between the first and second fingers of each hand. The other fingers should remain relaxed. Slowly stroke your hands alternately along the jawbone out toward the ears. As each hand reaches the ear, release and place the hand back on your partner's chin. Eating and talking both cause muscle tension and jaw stiffness, and this stroke is marvellous for relaxing tension around the jaw. It will also help people who grind their teeth in the night. However, if your partner has any loose teeth, or tooth or gum discomfort, then omit this movement completely.

2 The aim of this stroke is to keep the movements flowing and smooth. As one hand approaches the ear, the other hand begins the movement at the chin. Repeat the stroke two to four times, gradually increasing the pressure a little.

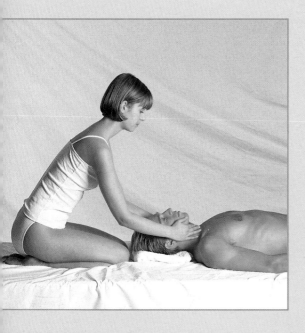

Stroking up the neck and sides of the face

1 Support your partner's head on a small flat pillow or folded towel. Your partner should close their eyes. Place your fingers very lightly under the chin so that your fingertips are resting on the neck. Be careful not to put any pressure on the throat area otherwise your partner may experience a choking feeling. Using your fingertips, slowly start to stroke across the neck and under the sides of the jawbone.

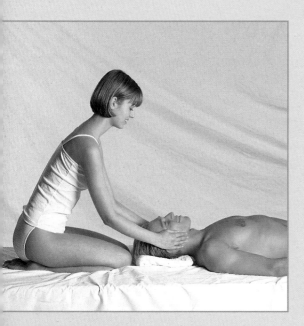

2 Continue to stroke under the jawbone and around the area just in front of the earlobes, adding a little pressure with the middle finger at this point to gently massage the lymphatic nodes. If they feel hard, or are sensitive to touch, avoid massaging them at all – this could be an indication that the body is trying to fight off an infection.

3 (right) Continue using your fingertips to stroke lightly up the sides of the face and over the ears, while visualizing the energy being drawn upward. Stroke gently over the cheekbones, then when you reach the temples increase the pressure with your middle fingers and pause while you massage the area. From here carry on stroking up the sides and over the top of the head. Continue to visualize energy and warmth being drawn to the top of the head and any stress being released. Use all your fingers to comb through the hair right to the ends.

Gently place your fingers back on to the neck area where you began, ready to repeat the whole movement. Repeat all four stages two to six times.

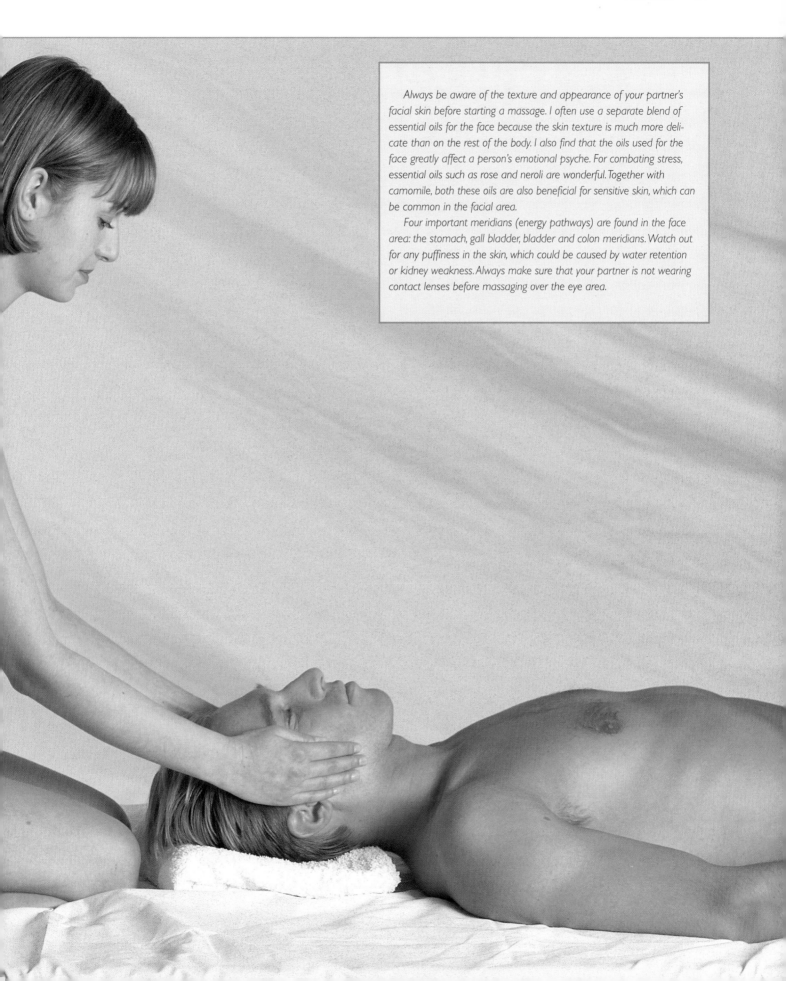

Always be aware of the texture and appearance of your partner's facial skin before starting a massage. I often use a separate blend of essential oils for the face because the skin texture is much more delicate than on the rest of the body. I also find that the oils used for the face greatly affect a person's emotional psyche. For combating stress, essential oils such as rose and neroli are wonderful. Together with camomile, both these oils are also beneficial for sensitive skin, which can be common in the facial area.

Four important meridians (energy pathways) are found in the face area: the stomach, gall bladder, bladder and colon meridians. Watch out for any puffiness in the skin, which could be caused by water retention or kidney weakness. Always make sure that your partner is not wearing contact lenses before massaging over the eye area.

The head and scalp

Head and scalp massage should follow a facial massage. All over the head there are reflexology points, which when stimulated can energize the whole body. By massaging the head and scalp you will be able to loosen the thin layer of muscles covering the skull. Massaging this area helps to increase the constant supply of blood needed by the brain and can promote deep relaxation.

Scalp massage has the additional benefit of increasing the supply of blood to the hair follicles. In India head and scalp massage is carried out regularly on both adults and children, using coconut oil to increase the growth and texture of the hair. Yogis stand on their head to increase the flow of blood to the brain and hair follicles.

Many hairdressers now train their staff to massage the scalp when washing a customer's hair, and it is something you can easily do for yourself at home, or even in the office. Make sure your nails are short because you will be using your fingertips.

Petrissage on pressure points
Your partner's forehead should be resting on their hands. Kneel at your partner's head and place your fingertips along the base of their skull. Ask your partner to take a deep breath in and, as they exhale, press with the pads of your fingers on the pressure points along the base of the skull. These are powerful acupuncture points, which the meridians pass through on their way up to the head. The base of the skull holds a lot of tension and gently massaging those points will help to reduce it. Repeat two to four times.

Finger glides

(below) Ask your partner to lie on their front and rest their forehead on their hands. Kneel just behind your partner's head and place your fingertips at the base of their skull. Slowly glide your fingers over the whole head from the bottom to the top. Once you have reached this point, release your hands and place them back at the base of the skull again. Repeat two to four times. This movement is wonderful for energizing the head and scalp, and can help to relieve headaches.

Thumb glides and finger circles

1 (above) Support your partner's head with a small pillow or folded towel. Place your hands on either side of your partner's head. Using the pads of your fingertips and thumbs, slowly rotate your right hand in a clockwise direction and your left hand in a counter-clockwise direction. Continue making small thumb and finger circles all over the top and sides of the head, extending down toward the ears. Repeat the same movement, but this time use finger and thumb glides all over the same area.

2 Turn your partner's head to one side and lower it on to the pillow or towel. Repeat the finger and thumb circles, this time reaching further round to the side of the head and the base of the skull. Turn your partner's head to the other side and repeat the movement.

The chest

The chest is the hub of the lymphatic system – all the toxic waste in the lymph fluid, which has been carried away from the lymph nodes, finally drains into the two main lymphatic ducts situated in the chest. The newly cleansed lymph fluid is then recirculated to the body through the veins in the upper chest. A great deal of tension can be stored in your chest, especially if your breathing is shallow.

Driving a car and using a computer are major causes of tension, because you are constantly poking your head forward and downward. Bad posture causes the muscles in the chest to contract, which in turn pull on the muscles in the upper back. A chest massage will help to relieve any tightness in the shoulder and upper back area. When massaging a woman it is best to massage the upper chest and rib area only, and not directly over the breasts. Keep the pressure fairly light. When massaging a man the pressure can be greater, as the chest muscles are usually much stronger. You may need to use extra oil for a man with a very hairy chest, to prevent pulling.

Effleurage
Kneel astride the top of your partner's head. Apply oil to their chest and place both hands on the middle of the chest so that your fingers are pointing in toward each other. Your arms should be slightly relaxed at the elbows. Take a deep breath in and ask your partner to do the same. As you both exhale, slowly effleurage your hands outward toward your partner's arms. Place your hands back on the middle of the chest, this time a little higher up. Repeat the breathing and effleurage so that you are literally "opening out" the chest. This is an area where we tend to hold on to emotions, so the combination of breathing and massage is extremely beneficial. Repeat the movement two or three times, working up the chest.

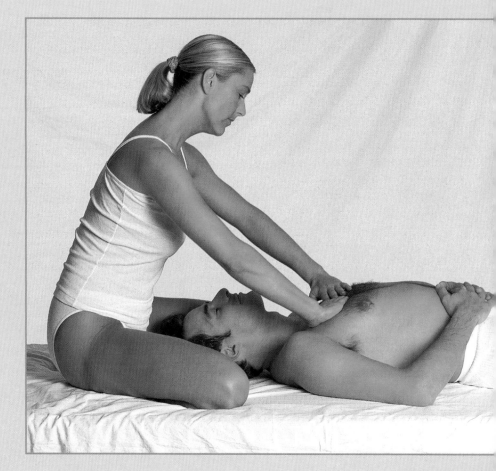

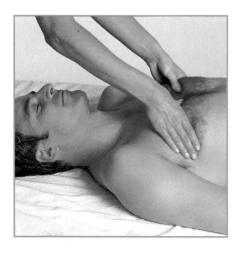

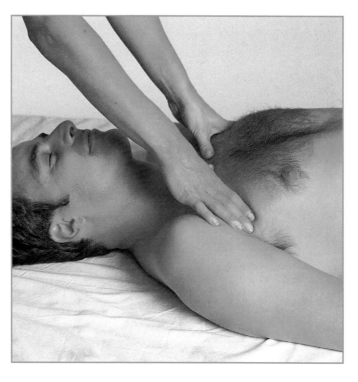

2 Place your thumbs back in the middle of the chest, this time a little higher up. Repeat the breathing, gliding your thumbs outward as you both exhale. Move your thumbs up the chest until you reach the collar bone. Both effleurage and thumb gliding can be beneficial for any congestion caused by catarrh in the chest area.

Thumb glides

1 Kneel astride your partner's head. Place the pads of your thumbs on the middle of their chest. Take a deep breath in and ask your partner to do the same. As you both exhale, slowly glide your thumbs outward across the chest toward the arms.

Knuckling

Kneel astride your partner's head. Make your hands into loose fists and place them on the middle of your partner's chest, so that your knuckles are facing one another. Using the same breathing technique as for thumb glides and effleurage, slowly glide your knuckles outward toward the arms. Provided the area is not too sensitive, you can use a little more pressure as you repeat the movement, gradually working up the chest. Repeat two to six times. This knuckling technique is useful for men who have well-developed chest muscles because it allows the masseur to work in between the ribs.

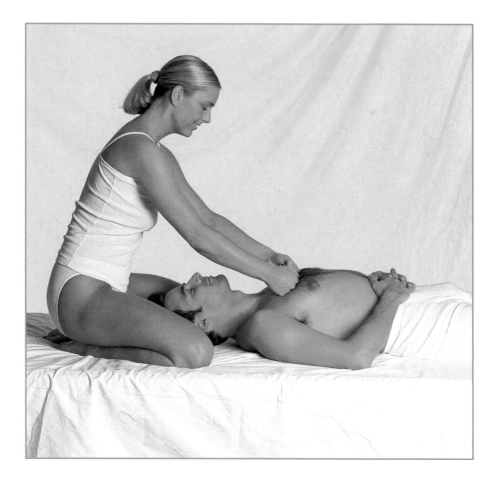

The arms

The structure of the bones in your arms is similar to that in your legs, but the bones are smaller and more delicate. The muscles in the shoulder stabilize the shoulder girdle, which then allows the arms and hands to move freely.

At first you may find the arms a little difficult to massage and it is probably easier to treat the upper and lower arms separately, as with the legs. Massaging the arms can release tension in the neck, shoulders and hands, and it can be extremely relaxing. Headaches and neck and shoulder problems can all be caused by tension in the arms and massage may alleviate them.

Arm massage is particularly beneficial for people who suffer from repetitive strain injury, or carpal tunnel syndrome. It is important that your partner totally relaxes their arm while you are massaging it. You should support the whole weight of the arm, or leave the arm resting alongside the body – though this may make it difficult to reach all of the muscles.

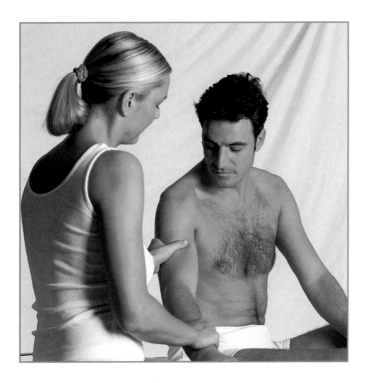

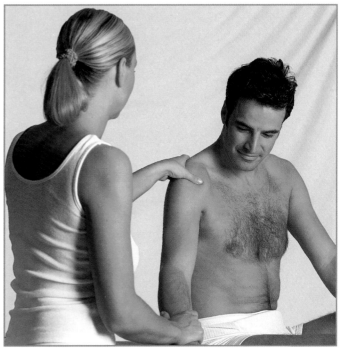

Thumb circling

1 For this movement your partner can either sit up or lie down. Whichever position is preferred, sit alongside them and support their arm with one hand while performing the movement with the other. With your fingers wrapped around the back of the arm, start to rotate the pad of your thumb in small circles above the elbow, over the biceps muscle and up toward the shoulder.

2 Circle your thumb over the shoulder joint, applying a little more pressure. Continue to massage the whole of the upper arm and shoulder until the muscles start to loosen. If your partner is lying down, you may prefer to perform this movement using alternate thumbs. You will still need to support the arm with your fingers underneath. Repeat on the other arm.

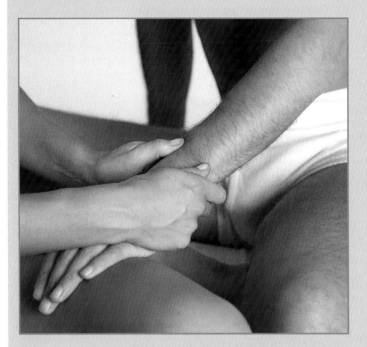

Thumb glides on the outer arms

1 Take your partner's left arm into both of your hands and rest their palm on your knee so that there is no strain on their arm. Slowly glide both your thumbs from your partner's wrist outward to the side of their wrist.

Thumb glides on the inner arms

(below) Take your partner's left hand into your right hand, allowing it to rest on your knee with the palm facing upward. Using your left hand to support your partner's arm, slowly glide the pad of your left thumb from the wrist all the way up to the elbow. The tendons in this area are often very tight, especially in tennis players, typists and musicians. Work on the whole of the inside of the lower arm area, then repeat the movement on the right arm.

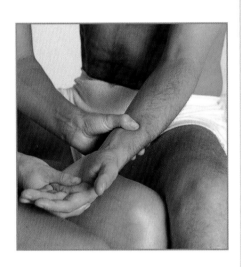

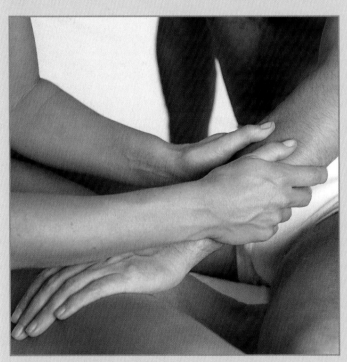

2 Continue the thumb glides from the middle to the outer arm, at the same time gradually moving upward until you reach the area just under the elbow. The muscles on this part of the arm are also used in many everyday activities and therefore benefit from massage. Repeat on the other arm.

The hands

The hands are one of the most sensitive areas of the body because there are thousands of nerve endings and, like the feet, they have many reflexology points. Hands are constantly exposed to the elements and to water, and the skin is thinner than elsewhere on the body, so they are one of the first places to show signs of ageing.

Most people love to have their hands touched, and they are easily accessible – you do not have to undress to receive a relaxing hand massage. We use our hands for almost every daily task, and people who use them constantly, such as pianists, musicians, typists, reflexologists and masseurs, benefit greatly from hand massage. The elderly, babies and children find a simple hand massage extremely comforting.

If you include a hand massage with a body massage, you can continue to use the same oil, but for a hand massage alone use a rich moisturizing handcream, which will also improve the texture of the skin.

Stroking
For this movement your partner can be sitting comfortably, as shown, or lying down. Sit on their right side and lay their right hand on your knee with the palm facing down. Support their hand with the fingers of both your hands, and place your thumbs on top. Starting with your thumbs in the middle, slowly stroke them outward as if you were trying to "open out" the hand. Move your thumbs back to the middle of the hand and repeat the movement a little higher up. Repeat two to four times and then turn the hand over to continue the movement on the palms of the hands. As there is more flesh on the palms a little more pressure can be used. Move to your partner's other side and repeat on the other hand. Many people find this movement very relaxing.

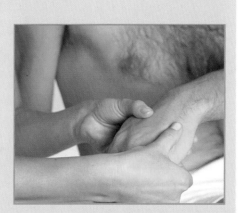

Thumb glides between the tendons
1 This movement can be carried out with your partner sitting or lying down. Sit alongside your partner and take their left hand into your left hand, supporting the whole weight. Place the pad of your right thumb between the knuckles of the third and little finger. Slowly glide your thumb in a straight line between the bones and tendons all the way up to the wrist.

2 Gradually move along your partner's hand until you have massaged between the bones and tendons of each finger. Finish by working on the space between the thumb and index finger. Important meridians run along these pathways, which is why they may feel sensitive.

Pulling the fingers

1 Sit on the right of your partner and take their left hand, with the palm facing down, into your left hand. Hold the base of their index finger between your right thumb and fingers and gradually massage the finger from the base to the tip, slightly pulling it at the same time. When you reach the tip of the finger, give it a little extra squeeze to stimulate all the nerve endings.

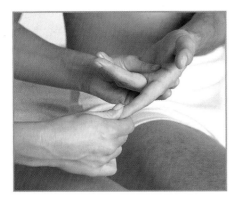

2 Continue the movement on each finger, finishing with the thumb, then turn your partner's hand over and massage on the other side. Repeat on the right hand. Provided that it is not too painful, this movement can be very beneficial in cases of arthritis and joint stiffness in the hands.

Hand clasp

To round off the hand massage sequence it is always nice to "ground" your partner by clasping hands with your fingers intertwined. This enables you to exchange energy and "open out" the meridians of the hands.

The abdomen

As with the buttocks, some people feel apprehensive about having their abdomen touched. This could be because they hold on to emotions in this area, and by allowing massage they may feel exposed emotionally. Oriental philosophies regard the abdomen, or *hara*, as the seat of consciousness because it consists of vital energy.

Within the pelvic cavity are the large and small intestines, and the reproductive organs – both very important parts of the body. It is important not to use too much pressure over this delicate area: gentle effleurage, stroking and circling movements are ideal. Massage on the abdominal area can benefit those who suffer from certain digestive conditions such as constipation, bloating and irritable bowel syndrome. It can also relieve premenstrual cramps, provided it is carried out gently. As long as there is no discomfort, it is perfectly safe to massage the abdomen during pregnancy. Massaging this area can be extremely soothing and relaxing.

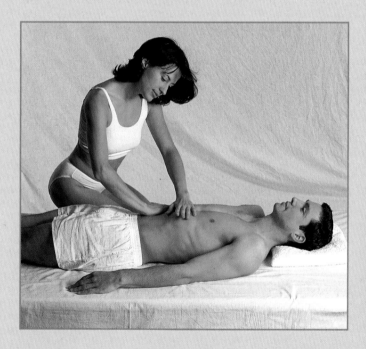

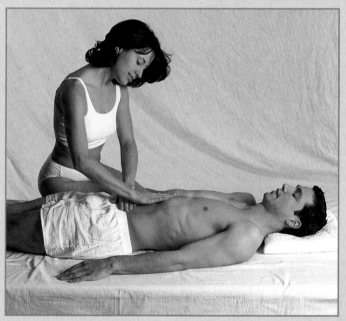

Circling

1 Sit or kneel to one side of your partner. Place both your lightly oiled hands on their abdomen with the palms facing down. Hold this position to make contact and generate some heat from your hands onto your partner's abdomen. Keeping the palms facing down, slowly sweep your right hand outward to the right, leading with the heel of your hand. Turn your right hand round so that the heel of the hand sweeps across the abdomen from right to left.

2 Sweep your left hand across the top of the abdomen as you did with the right hand in stage 1. Keep sweeping both hands over the abdomen in circular movements until they end up sweeping almost in a figure-of-eight shape. It may take a bit of practice, but the important thing is to keep the movements flowing and not lose contact with the body. This gentle movement can benefit digestive problems and premenstrual abdominal pain.

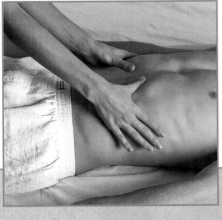

Thumb glides

1 Sit or kneel to one side of your partner. Place your thumbs together on the solar plexus just under the breastbone. Your fingers should be relaxed around the sides of the ribs. Ask your partner to take a deep breath in, then when they exhale press down gently with the pads of your thumbs and start to glide them down toward the navel.

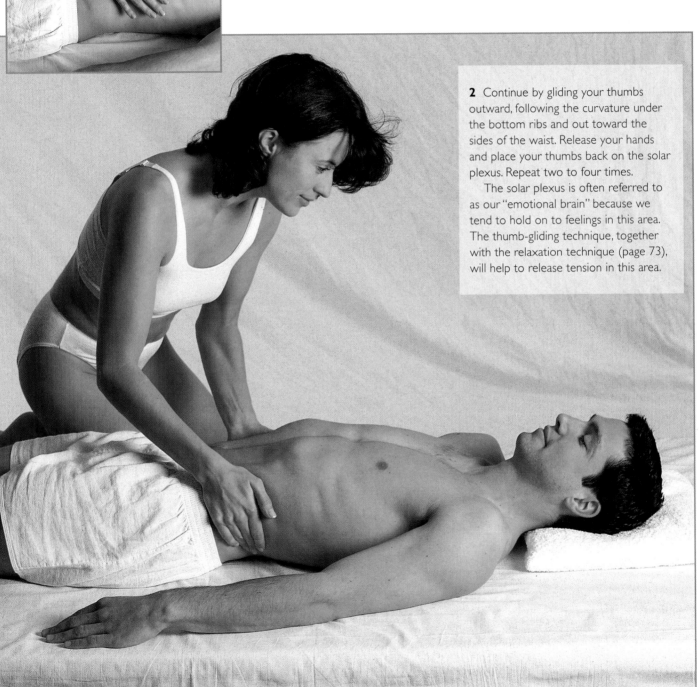

2 Continue by gliding your thumbs outward, following the curvature under the bottom ribs and out toward the sides of the waist. Release your hands and place your thumbs back on the solar plexus. Repeat two to four times.

The solar plexus is often referred to as our "emotional brain" because we tend to hold on to feelings in this area. The thumb-gliding technique, together with the relaxation technique (page 73), will help to release tension in this area.

Pulling from the waist

1 (right) Sit or kneel to one side of your partner level with their hips. Oil is not necessary for this movement, unless your partner's skin is particularly dry. Ask your partner to take a deep breath in and then perform the movement on the exhalation. Place both hands under your partner's waist as far as you can reach, with your palms facing up and your fingers pointing in toward each other. Slowly start to pull your hands from the back of the waist to the sides of the waist. At this stage you will have "opened out" the lower back area.

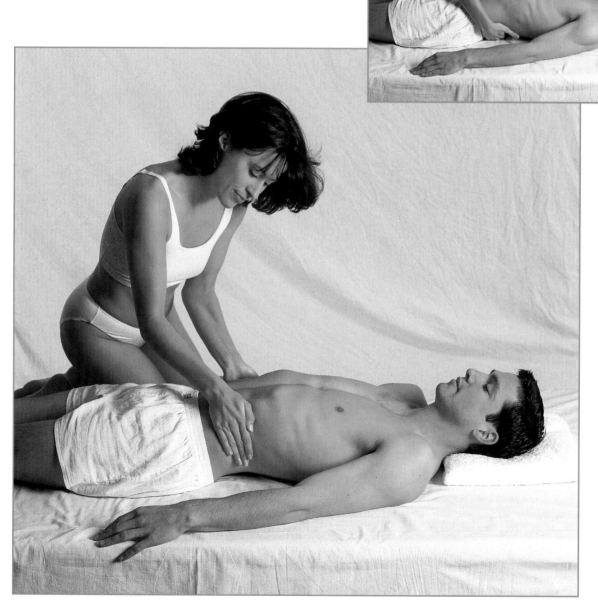

2 (left) Continue to pull both hands around the waist and over the abdomen, using your fingers to draw the flesh toward the navel. Once you reach the navel, lift your hands off and put them back under the waist. Repeat the stroke two to four times.

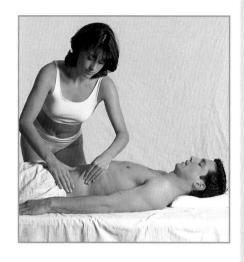

Kneading

1 (above) Sit or kneel to one side of your partner. Your hands should be lightly oiled for this movement. Reach across their body and place your hands on the far side of your partner's waist. Using your right hand, scoop up the flesh from the area between the ribcage and the hip with your thumb and fingers. Roll it with your fingers while pressing in with your thumb.

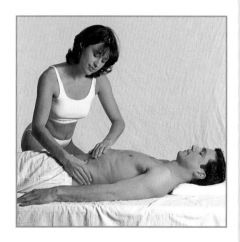

2 Repeat the kneading action with your left hand. Continue alternating both hands, keeping the movements small and rhythmical. Be careful not to pinch the skin and only use this movement on the sides of the waist, not on the abdomen itself. Kneading should be done after the area has been prepared by previous strokes.

Relaxation and breathing

Sit or kneel to one side of your partner. Place both your hands, palms downward and one on top of the other, on the solar plexus. Ask your partner to take a deep breath and breathe in yourself at the same time. As you both exhale, push gently with your top hand on the bottom hand to release all the air from the diaphragm and the tension from the solar plexus. Encourage your partner to breathe deeply in and out for a little longer as you repeat this relaxation exercise, pressing a little harder with your fingers each time.

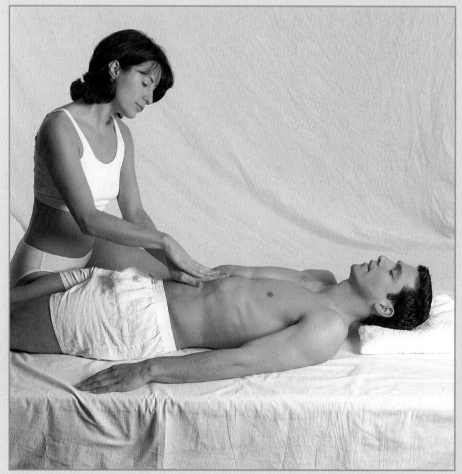

The fronts of the legs

We tend to be more aware of the look and feel of the fronts of our legs because they are visible when we look in the mirror or lie in the bath. The muscles are used at all times other than when we rest. If they become too tight, the muscles on the inner thighs can cause hip, knee or lower back (*sacro iliac*) problems. If these muscles are weak, this, too, can cause back problems because they are responsible for stabilizing the trunk. Many of the massage movements suggested here have already been outlined in the section on the backs of the legs (page 52).

Dancers, athletes and those who exercise regularly will particularly appreciate a leg massage, but anyone can benefit from massage in this area – the increased blood and lymph circulation will energize the legs tremendously. Be careful around the delicate knee area and use only very light pressure along the shinbone. If your partner has varicose veins, massage gently around the area and not over it. The upper leg will benefit from deeper pressure than the lower leg. Massage is very effective for breaking down stubborn fat on the upper thighs.

Cupped-hand effleurage

I Sit or kneel to one side of your partner. You will be working on the leg closer to you. Place your hands in the cupped position around the thigh about 3in (8cm) above the knee. Your fingers should be relaxed and close together, literally cupping the contour of the thigh muscle. Slowly effleurage one hand up the thigh so that the heel of your hand and your fingers are pressing gently in toward each other.

2 As the first hand reaches the top of the thigh, start the movement from the lower thigh with your other hand sliding up to the top of the thigh. Alternate the movement smoothly with both hands, rhythmically working over the whole thigh area. Change to the other side to repeat on the other leg.

Wringing

1 Sit or kneel to one side of your partner, facing their thighs. Open their legs slightly so that you can reach the inner part of the leg. Reach across your partner's body and place your hands on the far thigh about 3in (8cm) above the knee. Your hands should be alongside one another, with the fingers pointing away from you. Slowly push one hand forward around the thigh while at the same time pulling the other hand toward you.

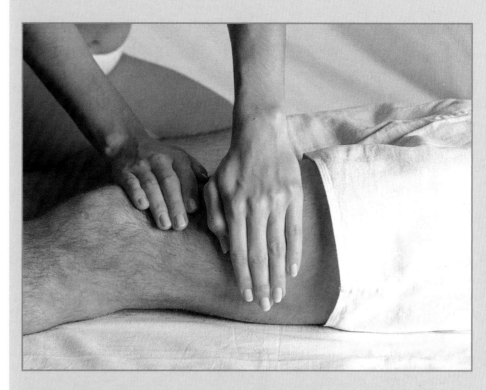

2 At this stage change the movement so that the pushing and pulling are done by the opposite hands. You should actually be able to see the flesh twisting beneath your hands as you lift it slightly during the movement. The more you lift it up, the easier it will be to wring. The degree of pressure will depend on your partner, but if you use your bodyweight to lean into the movement it will help to wring the muscle and not just the skin. You can stay in this position to massage the near leg or move to the other side. Repeat the movement, covering the whole of the upper thigh.

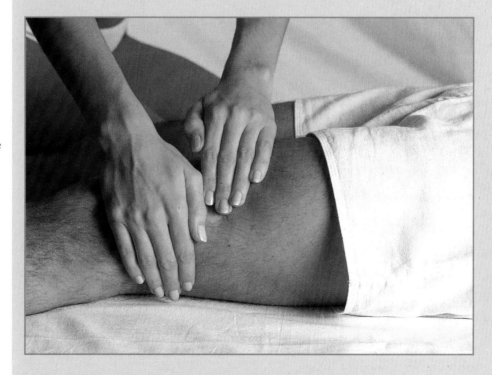

Kneading

1 Sit or kneel to one side of your partner facing their thighs. Reach across and place your hands on the upper thigh of the far leg. Scoop the flesh between the thumb and fingers of your left hand and squeeze and roll it before taking over with the other hand. Repeat the same action, squeezing and rolling the muscle in your right hand.

2 Alternating your hands, keep the movement continuous, working from hand to hand with a fairly slow and even pace until the whole upper thigh has been covered, with the exception of the area just above the knee. Repeat on the other leg. Do not perform this movement on very thin legs or on areas where there are varicose veins or broken capillaries.

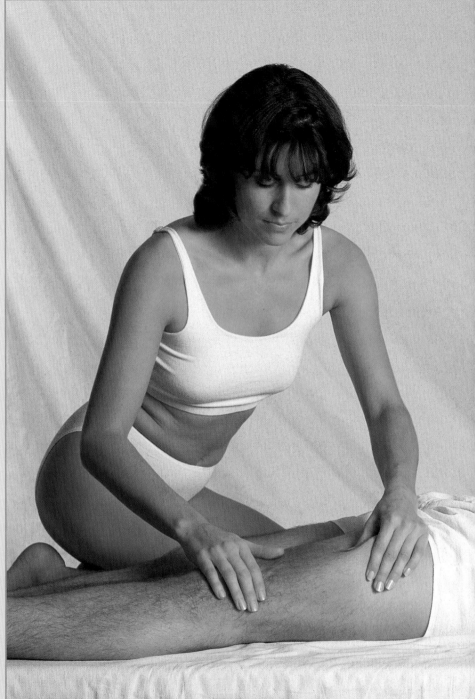

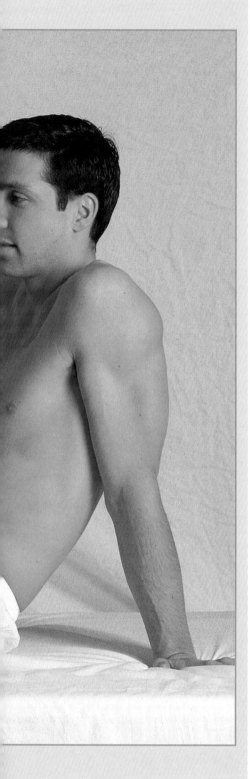

Knuckling

(right) Sit or kneel to one side of your partner ready to work on the leg nearer to you. With your hands in a loose fist, use your knuckles to massage the leg in an upward and downward movement. Slide your knuckles alternately up the thigh, starting about 3in (8cm) from the knee. This is particularly beneficial for people with large muscular legs because the movement can generate deep pressure. Do not use knuckling on varicose veins.

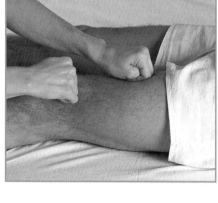

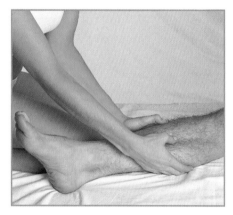

Petrissage on the shinbones

(left) Sit or kneel to one side of your partner level with their feet. Place your thumbs on one leg just above the ankle area on either side of the shinbone. Using the pads of your thumbs, slowly slide them up the length of the bone to the area beneath the knee. Release the pressure and place your thumbs back at the starting position. Never put pressure on the shinbone itself. Repeat two to four times on each leg.

Petrissage around the knees

Sit or kneel to one side of your partner level with their lower leg. Place the pads of your thumbs just above the kneecap with your fingers resting around the sides of the knee. Petrissage around the whole of the knee area by pressing with your thumbs for two seconds and then releasing. Never work over the kneecap itself. Repeat twice around the knee on each leg.

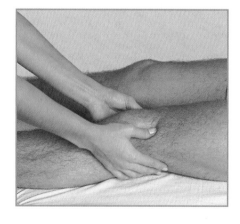

The feet

The feet are a very important, though often neglected, part of our anatomy. In an average lifetime they can take us the equivalent of five times around the world, and for this reason alone they surely deserve care and attention. Referred to by Leonardo da Vinci as "the greatest engineering device in the world", the foot consists of 28 bones and about 7,000 nerve endings.

There are numerous reflexology points located on the feet, which when stimulated through massage energize the whole body. Some feet are structurally very stiff and benefit from gentle rotation of the ankle in both directions. Rotation of the toes can also help to loosen the foot. Most people love to have their feet massaged, but if you find that someone is ticklish apply a more positive pressure. Foot massage can be both relaxing and stimulating: given as a treatment on its own it can benefit the whole body, leaving you feeling rejuvenated and as if you are walking on air.

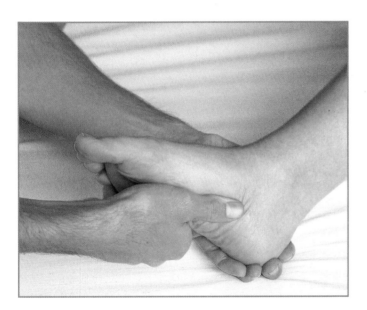

Thumb glides on the inner sides of the feet
(above) Take your partner's right foot in your left hand, supporting the heel with your fingers. Using the pad of your right thumb, begin on the side of the big toe, sliding your thumb down the inside of the foot. Following the line of the foot, continue the movement down along the side of the heel. Release your thumb and repeat again from the big toe. Repeat the movement, adding a little more pressure each time. Some areas may feel rather sensitive because this is the reflexology spinal area of the foot. Repeat on the left foot, using your left thumb.

Thumb glides between the tendons
(below) Take your partner's right foot in your left hand, supporting the heel with your fingers. Place the pad of your right thumb between the base of the big and the first toe. Slowly glide your thumb between the bones and tendons of these toes until you reach the top of the instep. Release your thumb and repeat in the same area, this time applying a little more pressure. Repeat the movement between all the toes of both feet. There may be sensitivity in some areas because you are working along the very important meridians in the feet.

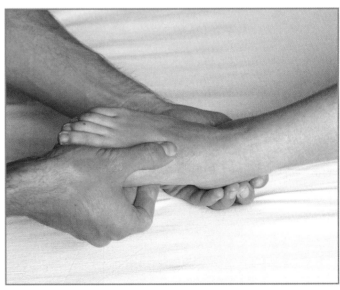

Knuckling from metatarsal to heel

1 (left) Support the heel and ankle of your partner's foot with one hand. Make a loose fist with the other hand and place your knuckles under the ball of the foot.

2 (below) Slide your knuckles right down the sole of the foot and over the heel. The heel is often a tough-skinned part of the foot and this technique allows you to massage deeply. Repeat the knuckling movement three to six times on each foot. If it is more comfortable, use the same hand for both feet.

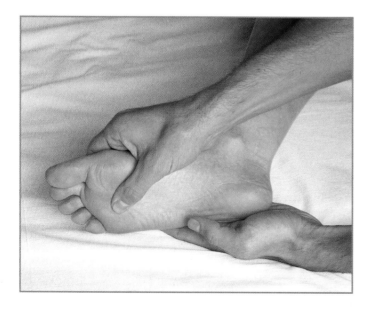

Thumb circles

Support the heel of your partner's foot in one hand and wrap the other hand around the foot so that the pad of your thumb rests on the ball of the foot. Slowly rotate your thumb in small circles, applying a little pressure at the same time. Gradually work all around and below the ball of the foot. Repeat on the other foot.

Pulling the toes

(right) Support the heel and ankle of your partner's foot with one hand. Clasp the top and bottom of their big toe between the thumb and index finger of your other hand. Pull the toe gently while massaging from the base to the tip. Repeat once again, applying a little more pressure. You can use the same movement to massage the sides of the toes. Continue working on each toe and repeat on the other foot.

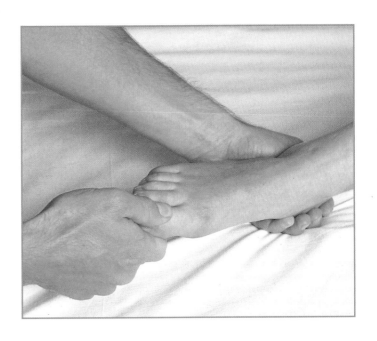

Stroking

1 Take your partner's foot between both hands so that the whole foot is cradled. Your top hand should face down and your bottom hand should face up. Hold this position for a few seconds then slowly start to stroke your hands from the ankle and heel toward the toes. Feel the contour of the arch with your bottom hand and the contour of the instep with your top hand.

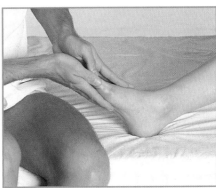

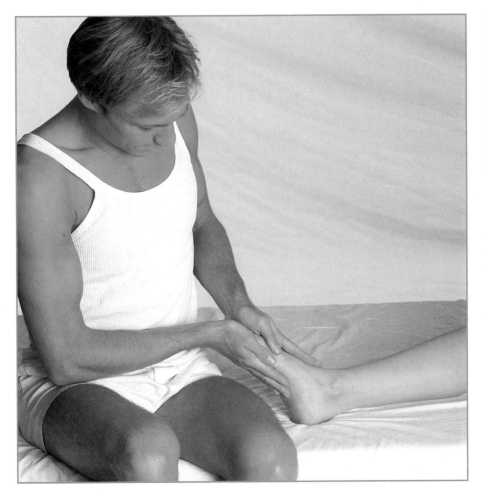

2 Continue to stroke the foot right along the tips of the toes, slightly stretching the foot at the same time. Mold your fingers to the shape of the toes as you stroke them and then very gently release your hands from the tips of the toes. Repeat the whole movement two to four times, clasping the foot for a little longer on the last movement. This is a wonderful way of rounding off the whole sequence of foot massage. Repeat on the other foot.

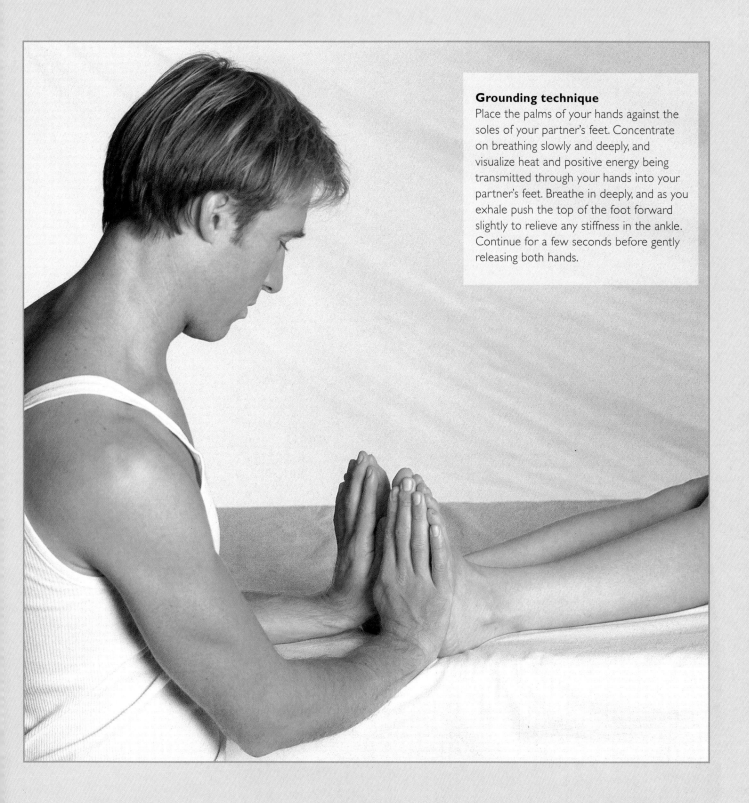

Grounding technique
Place the palms of your hands against the soles of your partner's feet. Concentrate on breathing slowly and deeply, and visualize heat and positive energy being transmitted through your hands into your partner's feet. Breathe in deeply, and as you exhale push the top of the foot forward slightly to relieve any stiffness in the ankle. Continue for a few seconds before gently releasing both hands.

the sensual
calendar

Nature is governed by the cycle of the seasons. With the coming of spring the sap of a tree begins to rise, feeding the buds until they blossom into summer leaves and flowers. When autumn comes, the sap reverses its flow and stores food in the roots to last during the winter sleep.

The cycle of seasons affects us as individuals, too. This chapter outlines our emotional and physical changes through the year and describes massages that will support our needs during each season.

The influence of the seasons

In earlier times rural life was governed by the seasonal cycle of sowing seeds, growing and harvesting crops, followed by the long dark winter months of candlelight and log fires. Today the seasons no longer rule our lives in quite the same way, but their influence still has a tremendous effect on our emotional and physical wellbeing.

Essential oils, incorporated into a massage or added to a bath, can help a wide range of "seasonal" conditions from winter depression to overheating in the summer. Use the chart on the opposite page as a guide for each season. The oils marked with two asterisks are widely available from health food stores and some pharmacies.

The less common oils marked with one asterisk can be obtained from the suppliers listed on page 144.

Some essential oils are suitable for more than one season. Lavender, for example, is a very versatile oil that has useful properties for a whole range of conditions. The essential oils of fruits are wonderful in the summer because they are so refreshing, but they can also be used in the autumn and winter for their uplifting properties, and they blend well with many of the spice and wood oils.

Whichever oils you choose for your massage or bath, they will certainly help you to relax, while at the same time revitalizing and healing – the natural way.

Spring

- Bergamot **
- Camomile **
- Cypress **
- Fennel **
- Gardenia *
- Geranium **
- Grapefruit **
- Hyacinth *
- Jasmine **
- Juniper **
- Lavender **
- Narcissus *
- Neroli **
- Rose **
- Rosemary **

Autumn

- Cardamom *
- Cedarwood **
- Cinnamon *
- Clove *
- Frankincense **
- Ginger **
- Lavender **
- Linden *
- Marjoram **
- Nutmeg *
- Orange **
- Patchouli **
- Rosemary **
- Rosewood *
- Sandalwood **

Summer

- Clary sage **
- Cypress **
- Geranium **
- German camomile **
- Grapefruit **
- Lavender **
- Lemon **
- Lemon-grass **
- Lime *
- Mandarin **
- Marigold *
- Melissa **
- Palmarosa *
- Peppermint **
- Petitgrain *
- Rose **
- Violet *

Winter

- Basil **
- Benzoin **
- Black pepper *
- Cajeput *
- Cinnamon *
- Coriander *
- Elemi *
- Eucalyptus **
- Ginger **
- Juniper **
- Myrrh **
- Neroli **
- Niaouli *
- Pine *
- Rosemary **
- Tea tree **
- Thyme *

Spring massage

Spring is a time of regeneration, renewal and vitality, when the long, dark days of winter begin to disappear. The trees blossom, the flowers come into bud, and bulbs explode into wonderful carpets of colour, their scent uplifting the spirit. This is a time for cleansing both the mind and body, and ridding the body of winter lethargy.

A fresh fruit and vegetable diet, dry skin brushing, lymphatic drainage massage and working the reflexology points of the feet related to the lymphatic system and kidneys, will all help with the process of detoxification. Simple floral essential oils such as camomile, rose, neroli, and lavender can be used to regenerate both body and soul.

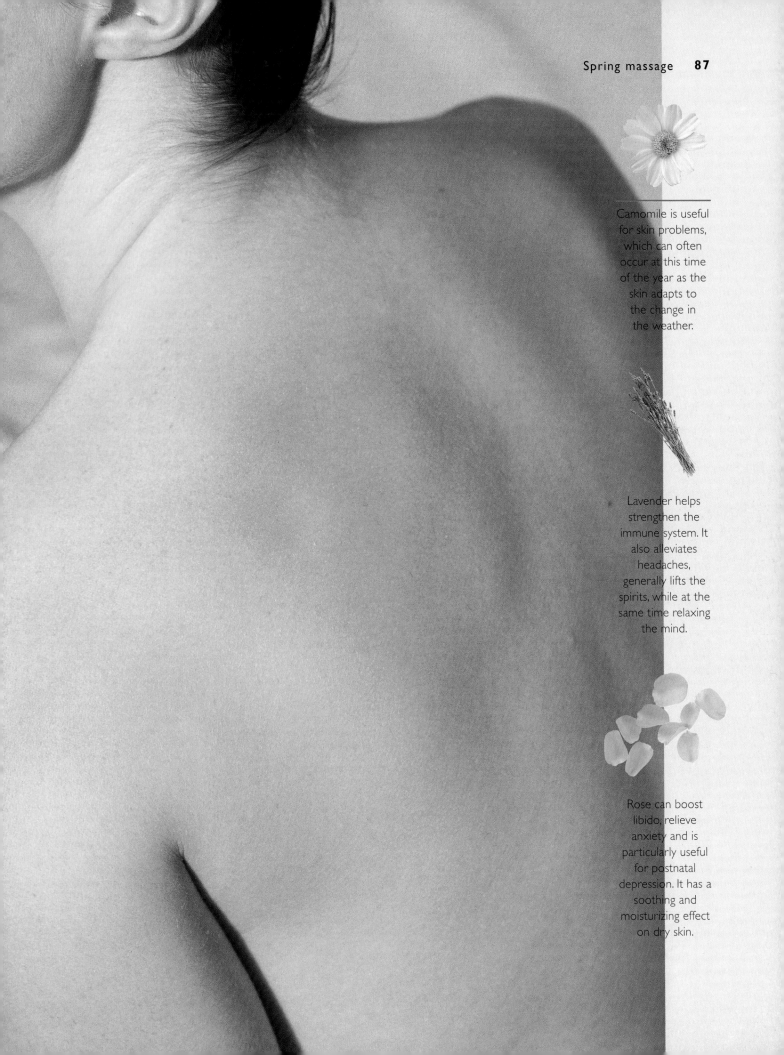

Camomile is useful
for skin problems,
which can often
occur at this time
of the year as the
skin adapts to
the change in
the weather.

Lavender helps
strengthen the
immune system. It
also alleviates
headaches,
generally lifts the
spirits, while at the
same time relaxing
the mind.

Rose can boost
libido, relieve
anxiety and is
particularly useful
for postnatal
depression. It has a
soothing and
moisturizing effect
on dry skin.

Cleansing the system

During spring we traditionally clean our houses and clear away the winter debris from the garden. It is also the perfect time to cleanse our bodies by encouraging lymphatic drainage. Lymph is a colourless fluid that circulates around the body carrying nutrients to, and waste products away from, the cells. Its movement depends on pressure on the lymph vessels from the activity of surrounding muscles, either through exercise or by massage. During the journey lymph nodes act as filters to prevent infection spreading into the bloodstream by neutralizing or destroying bacteria.

The largest lymph nodes are in the neck, armpits, elbows, groin and backs of the knees. The main lymphatic ducts are in the chest. Poor lymph circulation may lead to recurrent infections, fluid retention and cellulite. Combined with body brushing, lymphatic massage using essential oils of geranium, juniper, cypress or rosemary is beneficial for a sluggish system.

2 (below) Continuing the action of pressing and releasing, gradually slide the pads of your fingers forward a little at a time. The aim of this movement is to drain the lymph into the main ducts, which are situated in the chest. Having started at the top of the chest, the whole movement should move about 4in (10cm) downward. Place your hands back in the starting position and repeat both stages twice more. Remember that as you press you should be pushing your fingers slightly forward each time.

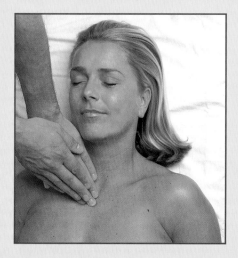

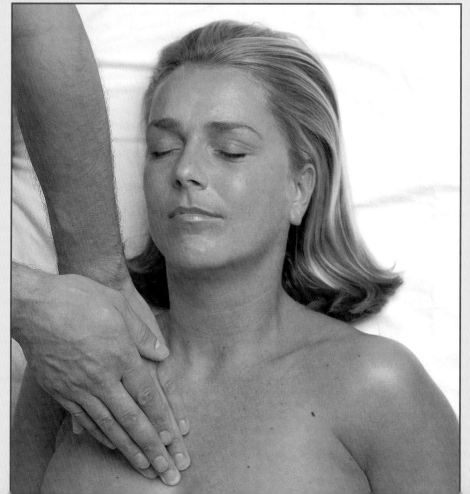

Lymphatic drainage on the chest
1 Stand or sit to the right side of your partner. Place your left palm downward at the top of the breastbone, then place your right hand on top. Your wrists should be relaxed, and the fingers not too rigid. Press your right hand down on your left hand for a few seconds, then release.

Stroking the forehead

1 Support your partner's head with a small pillow if it is more comfortable for them. Place your right hand across the forehead. Leave your hand in this position for a few seconds, then slowly start to draw it upward toward the hairline, using a gentle stroking action.

2 As the little finger of your right hand reaches the hairline, place your left hand on the forehead. Continue to stroke the forehead in an upward direction, hand after hand. Repeat the massage five to seven times, keeping the movement slow and rhythmic.

Petrissage on pressure points

(right) Sit or stand behind your partner's head and place one hand on top of the other with both palms downward in the middle of their forehead just above the eyebrows. Gently press the pads of the fingers of your top hand on to the underlying hand and hold for a couple of seconds before releasing. Remember that your fingers should not be too rigid. Continue the movement, slowly pressing for a couple of seconds and then releasing. Move your hands gradually up over the forehead until you reach the hairline. Release your hands then gently place them back at the starting position just above the eyebrows. If you wish you can change hands at this stage. Gradually move up the forehead, again gently pressing and releasing. Repeat the whole sequence four to six times.

Both the forehead massages work well for headaches caused by too much sun. When combined with essential oils such as peppermint or melissa (lemon-balm) they can have a wonderful cooling effect.

Cooling the legs and feet

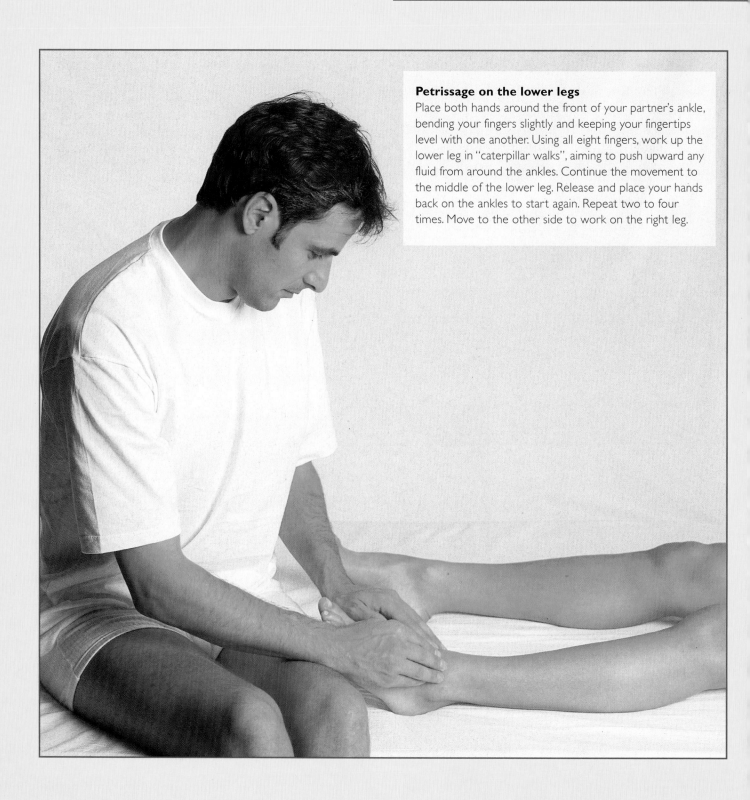

Petrissage on the lower legs
Place both hands around the front of your partner's ankle, bending your fingers slightly and keeping your fingertips level with one another. Using all eight fingers, work up the lower leg in "caterpillar walks", aiming to push upward any fluid from around the ankles. Continue the movement to the middle of the lower leg. Release and place your hands back on the ankles to start again. Repeat two to four times. Move to the other side to work on the right leg.

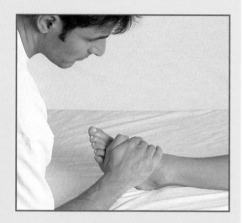

Effeurage on the lower legs

1 Sit or stand at the end of your partner's left foot. Gently bend the left knee, keeping the foot flat. Hold the calf muscle with your right hand and place your left hand around the area just above the ankle. Slowly start to effleurage your left hand up the leg over the calf, squeezing it a little between your thumb and fingers.

Effleurage on the feet

1 With your partner lying or sitting comfortably, sit or stand to the outer side of the left foot. Wrap your right hand around the left foot with your little fingers level with the ankle bone. Slowly effleurage down the foot toward the toes.

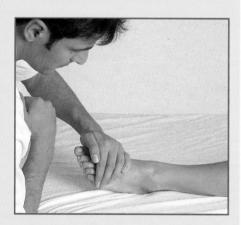

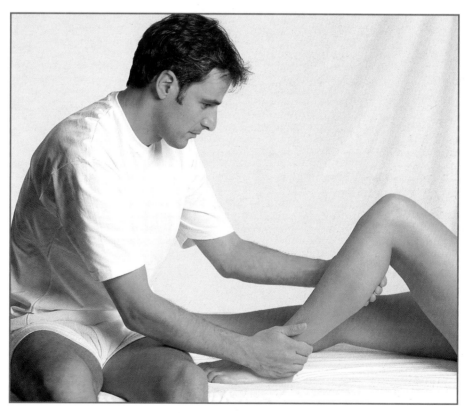

2 As your right hand nears the end of the toes, place your left hand on top of the foot in the starting position. Repeat the movement, gliding your hand downward. Continue to use alternate hands from the top of the instep down to the toes. Repeat six to eight times. Move to the other side to work on the right foot.

2 As your left hand reaches the top of the calf, release your right hand and place it just above the ankle. Repeat the same movement using your right hand. Continue to effleurage using alternate hands and cupping the calf muscle between thumb and fingers. As one hand performs the movement the other is supporting the leg. Repeat six to eight times, then move to the other leg.

Autumn massage

The autumn, with its gold and russet tones, can be the most beautiful time of year. It is the season of fruitfulness and harvest festivals, but also of dampness and decay. Flowers and plants wither away and the days shorten. The spirit can sink at this time of year, and many people suffer from seasonal affective disorder (SAD) owing to the decrease in daylight.

Resistance to colds and chest infections is lower in the autumn, and the damp air can exacerbate joint problems such as arthritis. An uplifting head, neck and chest massage to combat the damp air is wonderful at this time of the year. Use spicy, woody or fruit-scented oils such as cedarwood, marjoram, orange, rosemary, patchouli and sandalwood.

Marjoram can prevent symptoms of the common cold such as a sore throat, tickly cough and tight chest. Its warming and sedative properties aid restful sleep.

Rosemary is a good analgesic and improves poor circulation. It can also help to relieve arthritis and rheumatism, which are common at this time of year owing to the damp air.

Orange is a warming oil, capable of brightening up the dullest days. The sunshine needed for the fruit to ripen is evoked by the rich aroma.

Alleviating muscle tension

In the autumn vulnerable joints will feel more sensitive because of the dampness in the air, but massage can help to open out the muscles and relieve any contraction. Having your shoulders kneaded for a few minutes can be extremely uplifting, helping to alleviate muscle tension in the neck, and generating energy in the head to lift your mood. Combined with face tapotement (a light tapping on the forehead and cheeks), which stimulates the blood circulation, this can be a real tonic to the system.

As there are around a hundred acupuncture points located on the ears, massaging them can stimulate circulation to the joints and muscles and generally benefit health. The Chinese in particular are firm believers in auricular therapy to promote overall wellbeing.

For people who suffer from respiratory conditions caused by dampness, steamy inhalations using the oils of benzoin, eucalyptus, sandalwood, frankincense or marjoram will make deep-breathing easier.

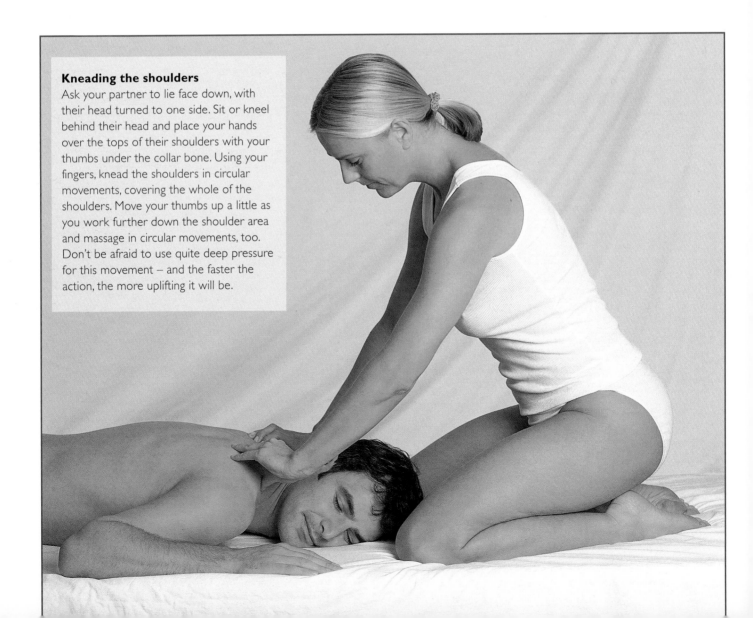

Kneading the shoulders
Ask your partner to lie face down, with their head turned to one side. Sit or kneel behind their head and place your hands over the tops of their shoulders with your thumbs under the collar bone. Using your fingers, knead the shoulders in circular movements, covering the whole of the shoulders. Move your thumbs up a little as you work further down the shoulder area and massage in circular movements, too. Don't be afraid to use quite deep pressure for this movement – and the faster the action, the more uplifting it will be.

Fan-stroking the back

1 (right) Gently turn your partner's head to one side and stand or kneel on the left side level with their hips. Place both your hands on the lower back and hold them still for a few seconds to make contact. Slowly glide your right hand up the back on the right side of the spine, slightly opening out your hand to the right side.

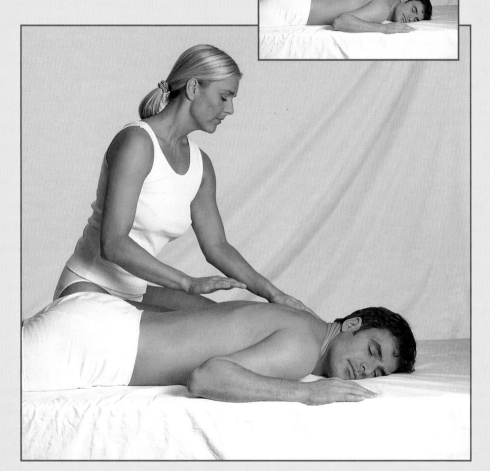

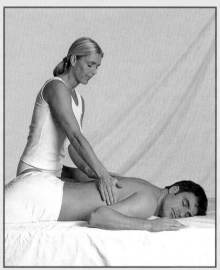

3 Continue the movement with your right hand, this time working farther up the back and over the shoulder blade. Open your hand out to the right so that your fingers fan out across the top of the shoulder.

2 Now repeat the movement described in stage 1 with your left hand. Glide it along the left side of your partner's spine, gradually opening out your hand to the left side. You will now have massaged the flat part and sides of the lower back.

4 Repeat stage 3 with your left hand, sliding it up along the left side of the spine and fanning outward and over the shoulder blade. All four stages should be repeated about four times, fanning the hand outward during each stage. Keep the movements slow and rhythmical.

Stimulating the circulation

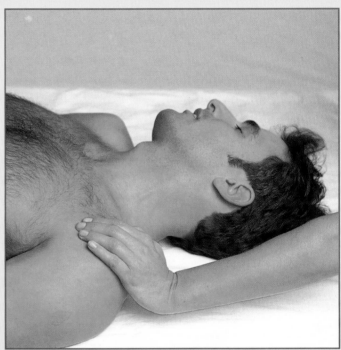

Stroking the neck

1 Kneel or sit behind your partner's head and gently turn their head to the right. Place the palm of your left hand on the side of the neck so that your thumb is directly below the ear. Gently stroke down toward the shoulder, being careful not to put any pressure on the front of the neck or on the throat area.

2 Continue to stroke down the neck and along the collar bone and top of the shoulder. As you reach the shoulder joint, press down gently so that you stretch the side of the neck and loosen the shoulder a little. In cold damp weather people hunch their shoulders without realizing it. This movement will help to relieve tension and loosen the shoulder. Repeat two to four times. Gently turn your partner's head to the other side and repeat on the right side of the neck.

Ear massage
(below) Sit or kneel behind your partner's head and place your left hand on their left ear, taking the lobe between your thumb and index finger. Gently rotate your thumb and finger over the earlobe. Gradually move up and around the whole of the ear, continuing the rotating movement. You will notice the ear start to redden a little – this is a good sign of increased circulation. Repeat two to three times then change hands to work on the other ear.

Tapotement on the face
Support your partner's head with a small pillow if it is more comfortable for them. Sit or kneel behind their head and place your hands gently on the forehead to make contact. With the tips of your fingers lightly tap all over the forehead as if you were playing a flute. This action increases the blood's circulation and is generally uplifting.

Winter massage

Winter is the season when animals hibernate, the soil lies fallow, the trees are bare and we tend to retreat indoors on long cold nights. Lack of exercise makes us feel lethargic and we are vulnerable to colds and muscular pains. Lack of daylight can lead to seasonal affective disorder. Massage is even more important during the winter than at other times of the year.

Essential oils of benzoin, eucalyptus, ginger, marjoram, frankincense, jasmine, black pepper, tea tree, rosemary and pine energize the body, uplift the spirits and warm cold and tense muscles. Facial massage can revitalize skin dried out by central heating, while hand and foot massage can warm the extremities.

Juniper is traditionally used as a tonic for a sluggish system. In winter it is particularly valuable for reviving the mind and body.

Ginger has warming, antiseptic properties that are beneficial for a whole range of symptoms from congested lungs to cold hands and feet.

Pine makes a wonderful inhalant for relieving chest infections, pneumonia and other lung conditions. Two drops in a bowl of hot water will clear any congestion.

Warming the lower back

The lower back often feels tight in cold weather and you may experience a "chill" on the kidneys. The Chinese believe that people who feel the cold in this area have a kidney deficiency. *Chi* is Chinese for "energy", and the massage described here energizes the lower back and generates heat around it. A hot-water bottle placed on the lower back can also feel warming and soothing.

The sides of the waist may also feel cold because body heat tends to circulate toward the middle of the abdomen where so many of the body's vital organs are situated. These areas can be warmed using the kneading technique. Cupping and hacking will stimulate the peripheral circulation and generally create warmth around the waistline.

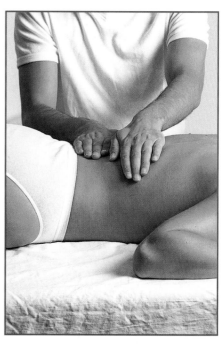

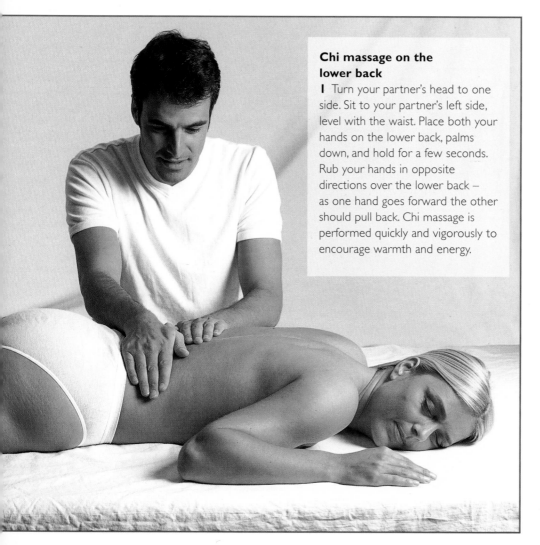

Chi massage on the lower back

1 Turn your partner's head to one side. Sit to your partner's left side, level with the waist. Place both your hands on the lower back, palms down, and hold for a few seconds. Rub your hands in opposite directions over the lower back – as one hand goes forward the other should pull back. Chi massage is performed quickly and vigorously to encourage warmth and energy.

2 Continue the movement until you feel some heat being generated from your partner's body. Be careful not to tense your own shoulders while carrying out this movement. You can perform chi massage without oil if you wish, or you can use one of the oils that are good for combating dampness in the bones, such as marjoram, cedarwood or rosemary.

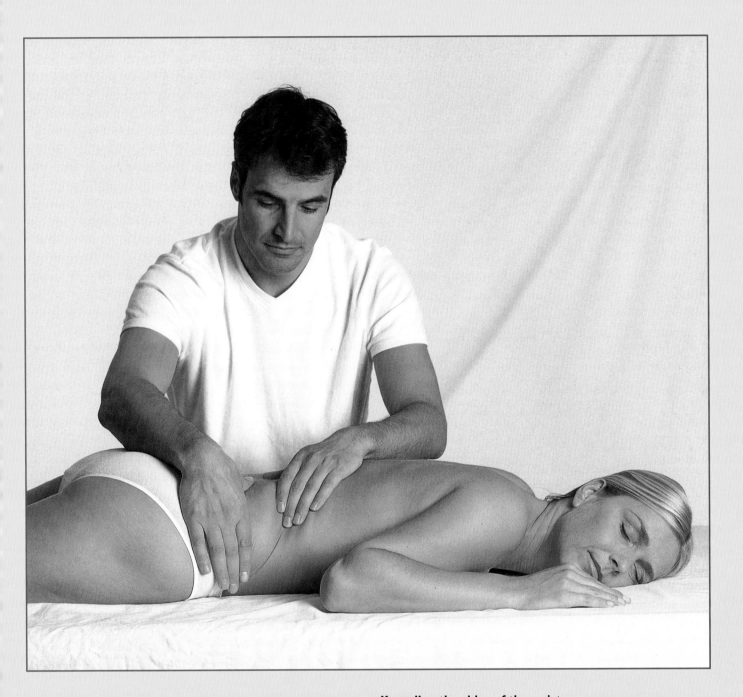

Kneading the sides of the waist

Turn your partner's head to one side and sit to the left, level with their waist. Place your hands across your partner's body on the right side of their waist. Take the flesh between your thumb and fingers and squeeze and lift it, using the kneading action. Continue the movement with alternate hands, keeping the action fairly fast so that the area becomes warmed. Move to the other side of your partner and repeat on the left side of the waist.

Warming the legs and feet

Massaging the feet

1 Ask your partner to lie on their back and lift their right foot in the air. Sit to the left side and place your hands on either side of the raised foot with your fingers over the sole. Support the front of the foot with your thumbs. Slide your right hand up toward the toes. Your fingers should remain bent as you use your fingertips to massage the area.

2 Keeping your right hand at the ball of the foot, slide your left hand down toward the heel. Continue the stroke by alternating the action, with your hands meeting in the middle of the foot and then continuing towards the heel or toes. By using your fingers to exert pressure, gradually increase the speed so that it builds up into a warming, uplifting movement. Repeat on the left foot.

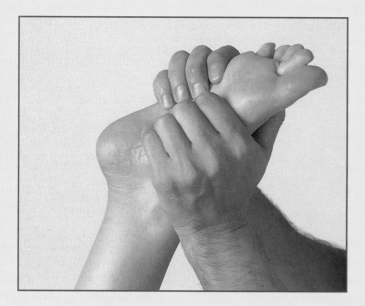

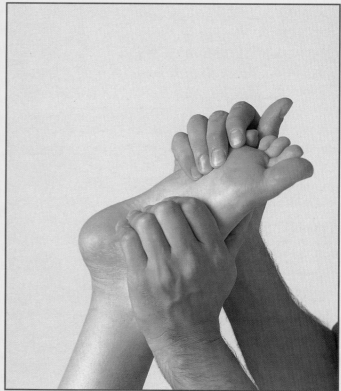

Cupping on the thighs

(below) Ask your partner to lie on their front. Sit or kneel to their left, level with their thighs. Working across the body on the right leg, cup your hands and alternately lower and lift each hand on and off the thigh. As you do this you are trapping air under your hands and increasing the peripheral circulation. Continue for a short while then repeat on the other leg. You can extend this movement on to the buttocks, if your partner wishes.

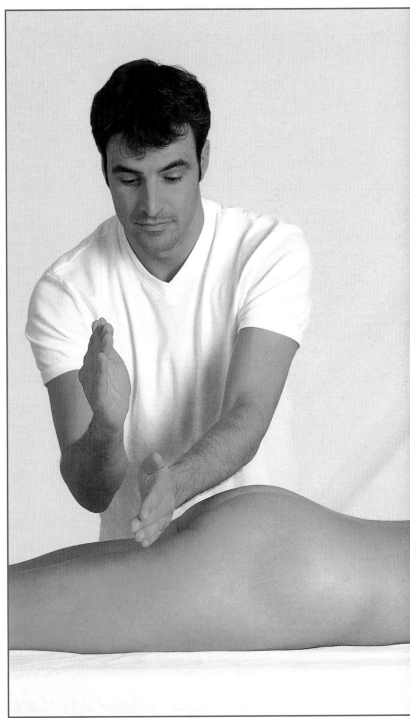

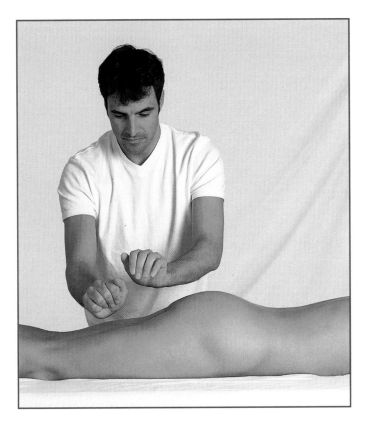

Hacking on the thighs

(right) Remaining in the same position, repeat the movement on the right leg, but this time with the hacking technique. Using the outside edge of the hands, alternately raise and drop them. Your fingers should be fairly relaxed – if they are too rigid the movement becomes too much like a chopping action. Continue using alternate hands over the backs of the thighs and buttocks. Repeat on the left leg.

the pleasures
of water

This chapter introduces you to the many pleasures of water, from simply luxuriating in an aromatherapy bath to "floating" into oblivion. You can enjoy the pleasures of a spa in your own home by following the suggested ideas for revitalizing the mind and body.

The sea is the perfect tonic for escaping the stresses and strains of everyday life. Sea air is fresh and full of moisture, so it has a cleansing effect on the lungs and skin. The pleasure of bathing in the ocean benefits both mind and body. The sound of the sea can generate a feeling of tranquillity and harmony – relaxation tapes of water sounds are widely available.

Relaxing the mind and body

Bathing in warm water lightly scented with essential oils is the perfect way to unwind after a stressful day. The healing properties of the oils soothe away anxieties and transport you into a state of relaxation.

Fill the bath with water that is pleasantly warm – if the bath is too hot, it can drain your energy rather than relax your body. Hot water could also cause the skin to become dehydrated, or damage fragile capillaries. Sprinkle

six to eight drops of essential oil on to the water and stir with your hand. Choose two of the following oils to aid relaxation: lavender, sandalwood, rose, camomile, jasmine, neroli or clary sage. Slip into the bath, close your eyes and visualize the stress being lifted from your body and mind.

Foot-baths

After a hard day on your feet, treat yourself to a foot-bath while you are reading or watching television. Remove any dry skin with a pumice or foot-file and then soak your feet for 10–15 minutes in warm water to which you have added a few drops of lavender oil. An old-fashioned mustard bath revives cold, tired feet: blend three teaspoons of mustard powder to a paste with a little water, add to a bowl of hot water and soak your feet for 15 minutes. Foot-baths can be especially beneficial for sufferers of arthritis or athlete's foot. If your feet need reviving, a quick dip into cold water that has been mixed with a few drops of peppermint or lemon oil will help.

Compresses

Compresses are good for relieving pain, inflammation and swelling. Add four to six drops of lavender, camomile or peppermint oil to a basin of water and dip a facecloth into it. Wring out and apply to the affected area. Use a hot compress for pain and a cold one for inflammation and swelling. Headaches, sprains and tennis elbow respond well to an ice-cold compress.

Creating your own relaxing and healing bath

Milk

Queen Poppaea, wife of Emperor Nero, journeyed with a train of asses to provide milk for her bath. Cleopatra also enjoyed the skin-softening and whitening properties of milk. Add one or two cups of instant dried milk to your bathwater and scent it with a few drops of essential oil.

Herbs

The curative power of herbs can be combined with water to relax the mind and body. Put herbs such as camomile, comfrey leaf, lavender or marjoram into water and boil for 30 minutes, then strain the liquid into your bath.

Oatmeal

This is excellent for sore cracked skin and eczema. Put some rolled oats in a muslin bag and hang it from the hot tap. Use the bag to scrub your skin – this has a mild exfoliant effect and can be useful as a soap substitute. Add some bran to the rolled oats for a cleansing and softening effect on the skin.

Vinegar

A cup of cider or wine vinegar added to your bath is wonderful for soothing dry itchy skin and easing aching muscles. Cider vinegar is also beneficial for sunburn and helps to restore the skin's natural acid balance.

Epsom salts

Made from magnesium sulphate, Epsom salts draw impurities from the skin and relieve aching muscles. Add 8oz (225g) of Epsom salts to a hot bath and soak for 20 minutes. When you get out of the bath, be sure to wrap up well and drink plenty of water because your body will continue to perspire and eliminate toxins for several hours. Epsom salts may also be added to a foot-bath to soothe tired and aching feet.

Bathing your emotions
Bach flower remedies help to soothe your mind. There are 38 remedies in total. The ones listed below may help you to deal with some common emotional problems. Add 10 drops to your bathwater, which should not be too hot.

- **Letting go of emotional ties to the past:** *walnut*
- **Exhaustion:** *olive*
- **Feeling in a rut:** *chestnut bud*
- **Inability to cope:** *elm*
- **Uncertainty:** *wild oat*
- **Loneliness:** *water violet*
- **Fear and apprehension:** *aspen*
- **Mental anguish:** *sweet chestnut*
- **Lethargy and depression:** *gorse*
- **Trauma and shock:** *rescue remedy*

With the exception of the rescue remedy, which is a special combination of five remedies, you can use two or three different remedies together in the bath, making 10–12 drops in total. In addition, sip a glass of cool water to which five drops of a remedy have been added.

The home spa

Water can have either a relaxing or an invigorating effect on the mind and body. In today's Western society we take ordinary bathing and showering for granted, but there are also all kinds of preventative and curative treatments available – some of which can be carried out at home.

Power showers

Power showers are available in most hotels and health-clubs, and can be enjoyed in your own home with the addition of a special pump. A power shower can stimulate blood and lymph circulation. When used on specific areas of the body, such as the thighs and buttocks, it breaks down fat and drains out any toxins. Alternate sprays of hot and cold water can restore tone to sagging breasts if carried out daily for about one minute. Brief applications of cold water from a power shower can also increase muscle tone and stimulate metabolic activity.

Jacuzzis

Most health-clubs, gyms, leisure centres and swimming pools include a jacuzzi in their facilities, and you can even have one installed in your own bathroom. The combination of warm buoyant water with the invigorating massage action of the hydrotherapy jets will increase your circulation and reduce stress on your muscles and joints, resulting in a relaxing state of weightlessness. Medical practitioners have verified the benefits of a jacuzzi for muscle soreness, back pain and even arthritis. A few minutes' relaxation in a jacuzzi can also relieve nervous tension and induce restful sleep.

Cold-water therapy

The restorative effects of cold-water immersion are not a new discovery – the Greeks first took cold-water baths to achieve "the harmony of their faculties through balance". Later the Romans developed a passion for wallowing in water at 64°F (18°C) to invigorate their bodies. In the 1850s two doctors developed cold-water treatment in the English spa town of Malvern. Although ridiculed by many of their fellow professionals, there was no shortage of distinguished names willing to vouch for the success of the treatment: Florence Nightingale, Alfred Lord Tennyson, Charles Dickens and Charles Darwin were all visitors to the spa.

A few years ago the Beatrice Hydrotherapy Research Centre opened in London to investigate, research and prove scientifically the effects of Thermo Regulatory Hydrotherapy (TRHT) and the benefits it can bring to sufferers of various illnesses. The research is under the direction of Professor Vijay Kakkar, a leading authority on thrombosis and circulatory disorders, and founder of the Thrombosis Research Institute of London. Professor Kakkar was a chronic asthma sufferer until he began a daily regime of cold baths.

So far research has discovered that cold water baths can boost the production of the blood-thinning enzyme TPA, which helps to prevent blood clots. When skin blood vessels are cooled, a number of hormones are released into the bloodstream, stimulating the thyroid and increasing the oxygen consumption of the blood cells. Cold water has been found to increase the production of white blood cells, which are vital for fighting off infection. It also stimulates the production of male testosterone, an important hormone that regulates sexual potency, and boosts estrogen in women, a hormone that is important in regulating fertility. Many people who previously had symptoms of chronic fatigue and related problems have also benefited from cold-water therapy.

Carrying out cold-water therapy at home

Anyone with a cardiovascular condition or diabetes should consult their doctor before attempting this therapy. It is important that you begin very gradually, so for the first two weeks fill the bath with water at a temperature of 68°F (20°C). The aim of the programme is to decrease the temperature of the water every two weeks, gradually increasing the length of stage 3, until you finally bathe in a temperature of 59°F (15°C).

1 Stand in the bath for five minutes – this allows the body to get used to the temperature gradually and also stimulates the reflexes of the feet.

2 Sit in the bath for five minutes.

3 Lie down for five minutes.

Stay on this programme for two weeks. Each day, add one minute to the time you spend at stage 3, until you are lying in the bath for a period of 15 minutes. For the next two weeks repeat stages 1 through 3 at 66°F (19°C), increasing the time spent at stage 3 as before. Continue to reduce the temperature every two weeks until you reach 59°F (15°C).

Water therapies

The use of water for therapeutic purposes is an extremely old procedure – it formed a major part of ancient Egyptian and Greek medical doctrine. The ancient Greeks believed that seawater had the power to cleanse the system of malignant tumours and to revitalize the nerves. Centuries later, when a German priest called Father Kneipp fell seriously ill he began to experiment with the healing properties of water. His personal success in curing himself encouraged him to recommend the treatment to others. Today his legacy lives on at Bad Worishofen and 600 Kneipp clubs throughout Germany.

Dead Sea magic

The Dead Sea has been renowned since ancient times for its beneficial effects: bathing places were built on its shores for Queen Cleopatra, King David, King Solomon and the Queen of Sheba. The waters were thought to have healing and beautifying properties.

This vast inland lake on the borders of Israel and Jordan is the lowest place on earth, lying 1,293ft (394m) below sea level. It is fed by the River Jordan and by numerous mineral springs. Because the area is very hot the water evaporates quickly, leaving a solution of mineral salts seven times more concentrated than other sea-water, in which it is impossible to sink. The mineral salts penetrate the body through the pores and have a wonderful therapeutic effect on the skin and on the body as a whole. They can detoxify the body, regulate fluid balance, increase blood and lymph circulation, calm the nervous system and speed up elimination.

The International Psoriasis Centre is based on the shores of the Dead Sea, where there are also many hotels offering spa treatments. Dead Sea minerals are available for home use as body and hair products, treatments for cellulite, and as bath salts. Add two to three handfuls of salts to your bath, then lie back and relax while the minerals restore calm and ease aches and pains.

Dead Sea mud

Mud baths, rich in dissolved mineral salts and plant extracts, were pioneered by the ancient Greeks. Today they are offered at spas and health farms as an effective way to clear out toxins, and treat rheumatism, arthritis and skin disorders. Mud is also a fashionable beauty ingredient: it is incorporated in skin-creams and certain salon treatments because it acts powerfully on the skin's

surface, drawing out impurities such as dead cells, excess sebum, and grime caused by pollution.

You can enjoy pre-prepared mud baths in your own home. When you use one for the first time it is advisable to soak for only 10 minutes, then gradually increase the time with each session. Mud treatments are not advisable for anyone who is pregnant or breast-feeding, or suffering from a heart condition, circulatory disorder, high blood pressure, diabetes, epilepsy or open wounds.

Thalassotherapy

Medical treatment using seawater is known as thalassotherapy, from the Greek word *thalassa*, meaning "sea". Seawater, plankton, seaweed and shellfish contain an abundance of natural components, such as mineral salts, trace elements, amino acids, vitamins and chlorophyll. All these elements are used in pharmacology, dermatology, dietetics and cosmetology.

Marine elements are indispensable for our biological equilibrium because each one of us is essentially a marine creature. The vitamins and minerals in seawater are almost identical to those in the body's own blood plasma. At body temperature these vitamins and minerals can enter into the bloodstream and be absorbed by the cells, thus rebalancing the whole body. The benefits of thalassotherapy are numerous: it can alleviate stress and fatigue; regulate blood pressure; purify the body; soothe muscular aches and pains; activate and regulate the hormones; speed up the metabolism; improve the quality of skin and hair, and even assist weight loss. Thalassotherapy treatments are available in spas and clinics, and in some countries seawater therapy is available on state healthcare schemes. Alternatively, there are numerous marine algae products available for use at home. If you are feeling tired or emotionally drained, or simply a little under the weather, a seaweed or sea-salt bath will help recharge your batteries by replacing necessary nutrients.

Flotation

Flotation is a way of promoting deep relaxation. It takes place in a cabin, or tank, filled 10–15in (25–40cm) deep with water at normal skin temperature. A mixture of Epsom and other mineral salts in the water supports your body so that you float.

A flotation session normally lasts for a minimum of one hour, and some people have been known to float all night. You float on your back with your head resting on an air pillow if necessary, and it is advisable to wear earplugs. While floating you can listen to gentle music through specially fitted underwater speakers, or you can relax in a completely soundless environment. You can choose to have a dim light, which you can control, or float in complete darkness.

Flotation provides the perfect opportunity for you to unwind and to meditate. Without the normal sensations of light and sound the brain tends to turn inwards, allowing a heightening of inner awareness. This, together with the therapeutic power of the mineral salts and water, enables you to float into a haven of mental and physical harmony and relaxation.

Watsu

A combination of water and shiatsu, watsu was started in California in 1980 by Harold Dull, a poet. Dull studied shiatsu in Japan, and when he returned to America he encouraged people to do shiatsu moves and stretches while floating in warm water. He found that they could move beyond their normal limitations because of the warmth and support provided by the water.

The basis of a watsu session is the freeing of the spine. The practitioner supports your body while you are floating and totally relaxed, and this opens up the energy paths of the spine. Stretching and rotating the arms opens up the related meridians. This continual flow of energy enables you to let go of mental and physical tension. Watsu helps a variety of problems: it can reduce stress, improve posture, increase the range of movement, improve sleeping patterns, increase energy, improve breathing and lessen muscle pain.

In ancient Egypt it was said that water is given to the soul as compensation for taking on a bodily form. In water our bodies find the freedom the soul has lost. Watsu is the continuing exploration of that freedom.

To do watsu at home

1 *Fill the bath with warm water (95°F/35°C).*

2 *Lie back and let yourself relax.*

3 *Feel the tension in your neck, back and joints being released.*

4 *Feel the warmth of the water penetrating your muscles.*

5 *Feel the stretch right through your body.*

6 *Visualize yourself floating.*

Purifying and toning the skin

Skin has many important functions: it regulates body temperature, provides a waterproof protective covering, serves as an excretory organ, and produces vitamin D. It is constantly subjected to dirt, smoke and air pollutants, which over the years take their toll on the appearance of the skin by clogging the pores, and introducing liver spots and fine wrinkles. To purify your skin eat plenty of fresh fruit and vegetables and drink 2–3 pints (1–1.5 litres) of water a day – this will benefit the body from the inside out. Equally important is skincare from the outside, and water plays a valuable role in this, too.

Saunas and steam baths

Saunas and steam baths have been popular in Scandinavia for many years as good ways of opening the pores and cleansing the skin. Wait at least two hours after a meal before taking a sauna and never drink alcohol just before or afterward. It is best to start gradually, beginning with five minutes and building up slowly. Always follow the sauna with a cool shower or plunge pool. A sauna soothes aching muscles, refreshes the mind, and may speed up an anti-cellulite programme. Never take a sauna if you suffer from a respiratory condition, heart disease or high blood pressure. Some people prefer to use a steam room or cabinet because the heat is less dry.

Give your face a purifying treatment at home with a facial sauna, or simply by steaming it over a saucepan of boiling water with a towel over your head. You can add your own combination of essential oils to the water: for normal skin add two drops of lavender and bergamot; for dry skin use rose and frankincense; and for greasy skin use geranium and lemon. Hold your face in the steam for a few minutes until your face starts to sweat, pat the skin dry gently and then repeat. Anyone with delicate skin prone to broken veins should avoid facial steaming as it could further weaken the capillary walls.

Once you have used steam and sauna on the face or body your skin is now nicely prepared for exfoliation, toning and moisturizing.

Exfoliation

The shedding and renewing of skin is a natural regenerative process that occurs on a three- to four-week cycle. As we age, the cycle lengthens and the skin can start to look grey, but by body brushing and exfoliation it is possible to accelerate the renewal process and achieve a more radiant skin. Exfoliation is like a gentle form of sandpapering to produce a smooth surface. There are many exfoliating products for both the face and body. When using an exfoliator on the face, be careful not to scrub too hard, and only use it once or twice a week. If you suffer from acne or pimples, avoid exfoliation completely.

A gentle, all-purpose facial scrub can be made at home by using one part almond oil to two parts finely ground oatmeal. Combine the ingredients into a paste and apply with your fingertips in small circular movements, avoiding the delicate eye area. After a few minutes rinse off with warm water.

Wet-skin brushing

Loofahs, bath mitts and body-scrub gloves are useful bathroom accessories for exfoliating dead skin cells. They can be used with water alone, or combined with an

exfoliating gel or scrub. Alternatively, you may prefer to use your own brand of shower gel. By adding a couple of drops of essential oil – rosemary, juniper, lemon, grapefruit, cypress or mandarin – you will create an even more invigorating sensation. Wet-skin brushing is a good way of removing excess dirt and oil, stimulating the circulation and loosening ingrowing hairs on legs.

Dry-skin brushing

As preparation for some of the more vigorous water treatments nothing works quite so well as dry-skin brushing. A natural-bristle brush swept over your body before a bath or shower stimulates the lymphatic system, clears the skin of dead cells and boosts the peripheral circulation. Always begin at the feet, using upward sweeping movements toward the heart and then down from the shoulder blades to the chest. Avoid the face, be careful over the breast area, and avoid patches of broken or irritated skin. Repeat twice weekly. Cellulite will also benefit from dry-skin brushing if combined with a healthy diet.

Sea-salt rubs

Sea salt works wonderfully as an exfoliator for removing dead cells and softening skin, especially on areas prone to dryness such as the elbows, knees and heels. Fill the bath with warm water and add 1–2lb (450–900g) of sea salt. Immerse yourself for about 10 minutes, then using a loofah or bath mitt brush upward over your body in the same way as for dry-skin brushing. Follow with a cold shower for a really invigorating feeling. If you prefer a shower to a bath, wet your body under a warm-to-hot shower, apply sea salt to your loofah or bath mitt and rub all over your body. If you have particularly dry skin, try a salt-and-oil rub by first dipping the bath mitt into olive oil and then into coarse sea-salt. Rub vigorously over the body and rinse thoroughly, following with a cold-water shower for added exhilaration. Apply lashings of body lotion or moisturizer after the treatment.

Face and body masks

For a deep-cleansing, toning and stimulating effect on the skin, a face mask can work wonders, provided it is the correct one for your skin type. For an oily skin use the deep-cleansing variety; for a dry and sensitive skin choose a moisturizing and hydrating one; combination and normal skin will benefit from a hydrating and replenishing mask.

Clay masks are based on kaolin, green clay (this can be difficult to obtain), and fuller's earth. All three are suitable for all skin types, although fuller's earth is particularly beneficial for oily and pimply skin. Add enough water to thicken the clay into a paste that you can easily apply to the face, avoiding the eyes and lips. Adding two drops of essential oil will give the mask a pleasant aroma. Leave on for at least five minutes and then thoroughly rinse off with warm water.

Many face masks can be applied around the eye area, and some are designed specifically for this part of the face. However, if you want to avoid your eyes, place a thin slice of cucumber or a cold used teabag over each eye to reduce any puffiness. Face masks should be used twice a week unless otherwise advised.

Body masks are also beneficial but very difficult to use at home. At specialized beauty salons and health farms there are a range of body treatments such as seaweed wraps and mud body masks, all of which contain deep-cleansing and detoxifying properties. Some beauty salons offer a back mask for spotty backs and foot masks for reviving tired feet. Hairdressers often use hair masks to treat scalp and hair conditions.

Toning and freshening

The next step in purifying the skin is freshening with a toner or astringent to dissolve any lingering traces of grime. Astringents are usually alcohol-based and should only be used on very oily skin. Rosewater, which can be purchased cheaply from any pharmacist, is refreshing for dry, normal and sensitive skins. If you are prone to spots, use a mild dilution of cider vinegar in a spray bottle of pure mineral water (be sure to keep your eyes closed when spraying your face).

It is easy to make your own aromatic waters by adding four to six drops of lavender, rose, sandalwood, orange, patchouli, peppermint or vetivert oil to a small bottle of spring water. Shake vigorously and apply with a cotton-wool pad, or with a spray bottle spray directly on to your face and body for all-over freshness. For an astringent effect add a little cider vinegar to your blend.

Toning bath

If you want to feel energized after a bath, the important things to remember are not to have the water too hot and to use a suitable oil. For an invigorating bath add three to six drops of essential oils of pine, basil, rosemary, coriander, nettle, orange, grapefruit, lemon-grass, mandarin, bergamot or tea tree. You can use just one of the suggested oils, or two together. To make up a natural invigorating bath extract, brew a pot of nettle tea then add a handful of fresh rosemary. Steep the mixture for 15 minutes, strain and add to the bath. Alternatively, add fresh pine needles and cones to a large pan of water; bring to the boil, cover and simmer for about half an hour. Add the extract to your bathwater.

Whichever method you choose for your invigorating bath, you should spend a shorter amount of time in it than you would in a relaxing bath. Ten minutes is the most you should spend, compared with 20 minutes for a more relaxing bath.

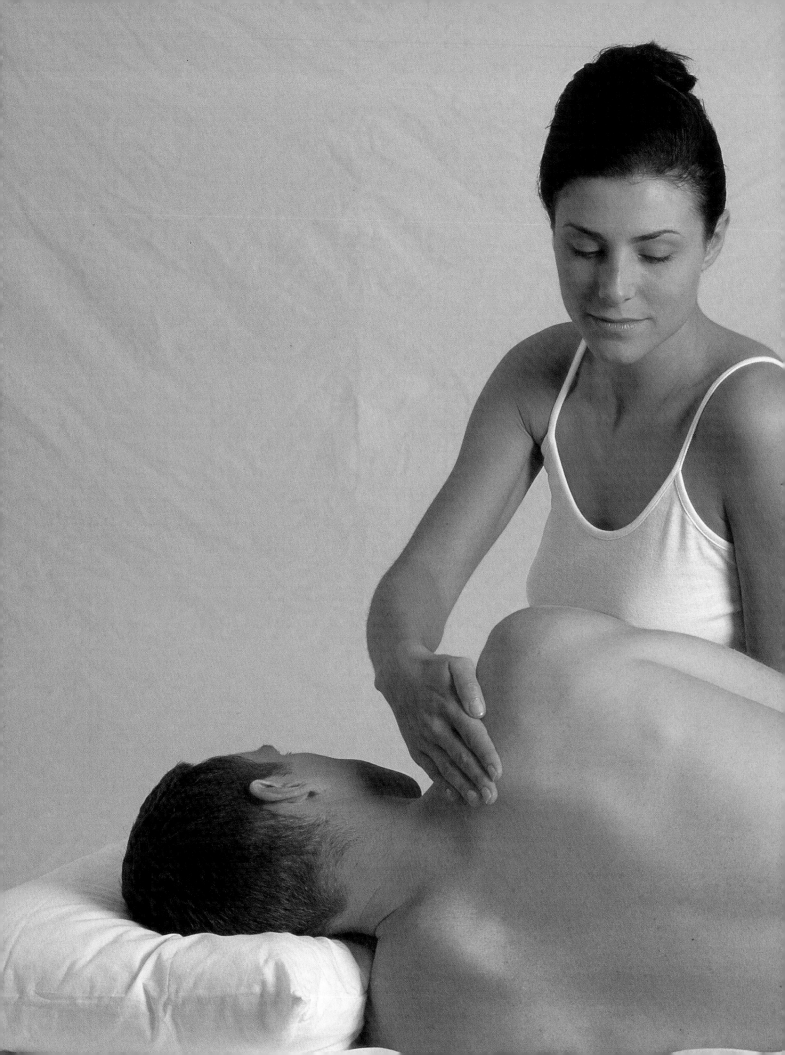

stress management through touch

Stress is an unavoidable aspect of modern living. Pressures at work, family tensions and bad nutrition all take their toll on the mind and body. Stress responds particularly well to massage. This chapter explains some of the stress-related symptoms that can occur, and suggests various massage techniques and aromatherapy oils that may help.

An Indian head massage normally incorporates the head, face, neck and shoulders, but the selected strokes described here are useful for overcoming anxiety. Self massage is also a wonderful stress-reliever, as well as a treat that you can give yourself. Taking active steps to reduce stress will pave the way for a more harmonious and healthy lifestyle.

The healing touch

Ageing is the result of the sum of all the stresses to which a person has been exposed during a lifetime.
Hans Seyle, Austro-Hungarian scientist who developed a Theory of Stress.

No one is immune to stress, and a certain amount can be good for motivation and heightened awareness. But too much stress can in the long term be destructive to health, placing an excessive strain on the mind and body. Stress-associated symptoms include headaches, migraines, sweating, palpitations, dry mouth, frequent urination, and digestive problems such as irritable bowel syndrome (IBS).

It is not always easy to recognize the causes of stress. It can be the result of psychological factors such as anxiety or depression, perfectionism, always being under pressure with deadlines to meet, trying to do more than one thing at a time, or feeling out of control. Environmental factors can also trigger a stress response: our bodies are constantly having to cope with the effects of potentially harmful substances in alcohol, cigarettes, exhaust fumes, medical drugs, coffee and a number of naturally-occurring toxins in food. In the past decade around 6,000 new chemicals have been introduced into our food, our homes and the world around us. Research has shown that exposure to these chemicals can induce both mental and physical stress, and eventually trigger a whole range of illnesses. A

The Turkish bath has been an important part of life in Asian countries for many centuries. Here (top left) a masseur is performing an Indian head massage.

recurrence of symptoms such as headaches and digestive disorders is quite often stress-related and should be addressed.

Just like a machine, our bodies "burn out" under too much pressure and need to be cared for and nurtured. Take time to relax and practise deep breathing and relaxation; give your mind and body time to slow down and recharge, and try to include a massage session each week before the stress levels build up. The following conditions may be helped by massage, using the suggested essential oils.

Essential oils for stress conditions

Allergies

Lavender, camomile and melissa oils are all soothing and can be used for massage, inhaled, added to baths, or used as skin lotions, depending on the type of allergy.

Anorexia

Lavender, neroli, ylang-ylang, clary sage and camomile have a calming and anti-depressant effect. Bergamot can help to regulate the appetite, and it has a generally uplifting effect.

Asthma

Lavender, camomile, bergamot, neroli and rose are all anti-spasmodic and anti-depressant oils. Frankincense can alleviate chest congestion. Deep-breathing exercises and massage will provide all-round help for this condition.

Cystitis or frequent urination

Camomile, eucalyptus, lavender, bergamot or sandalwood can be used to massage the lower abdomen or added to the bath. Garlic oil capsules are also beneficial.

Depression

Lavender, clary sage (not to be combined with drink or alcohol because it can induce bad dreams), camomile, ylang-ylang and sandalwood are all sedative and anti-depressant. Bergamot, geranium, melissa and rose are uplifting to the spirit. Neroli and jasmine are both calming antidotes for anxiety.

Eczema

Camomile, lavender, melissa and neroli may be used for massage or added to baths. Dead Sea salts (see page 116) are also beneficial.

Hair loss

Massage the scalp with olive or almond oil. Add a little rosemary oil to your shampoo if you have dark hair.

Headaches and migraines

Apply lavender or peppermint oil neat on each temple or in a cold compress placed on the forehead. Alternatively, add a few drops to a saucepan of hot water, put a towel over your head and inhale. A few drops may also be added to a handkerchief or tissue.

Heart disease

Lavender, rosemary, rose, marjoram or peppermint are believed to have a strengthening effect on the heart. Garlic oil capsules taken internally are also beneficial.

High blood pressure

Lavender, marjoram and ylang-ylang are all beneficial. Neroli and ylang-ylang are particularly effective for shortness of breath or palpitations.

Indigestion

Try massaging your abdomen with camomile, lavender, fennel, marjoram or peppermint oil. Camomile, fennel and peppermint can also be drunk as teas.

Insomnia

Lavender, neroli, camomile, marjoram and sandalwood are beneficial. Use them in massage, add them to the bath, or put a few drops on your pillow at night.

Loss of libido

Oils of ylang-ylang, patchouli, rose, jasmine, neroli or sandalwood may help this problem.

Conquering stress

Indian head massage

Based on the traditional form of *champi* (head massage) practised in India for more than 1000 years, Indian head massage is a simple, safe and effective therapy for combating stress. Champissage is commonplace in India, as the techniques have been preserved and passed down through generations over the centuries. Mothers teach their children from an early age. There is no need to undress and no oil is used, so you can give or receive an Indian head massage anywhere.

If you book an appointment for an Indian head massage it will invariably include the neck, shoulders, face, scalp and ears. The head, neck and shoulders are the energy centres of your body. If you are feeling stressed or angry, tension tends to manifest itself in a stiff neck or shoulders, in eyestrain or occasionally loss of hair. Head massage stimulates and improves scalp circulation, strengthens and improves the texture of the hair and increases its rate of growth. Mentally it can induce a feeling of calmness and tranquillity, help the recipient to think more clearly, relieve anxiety, improve concentration and alleviate mental tiredness.

The strokes described here can be performed at home on your partner. Be careful not to push down too much on their head, as this might cause pressure on the neck.

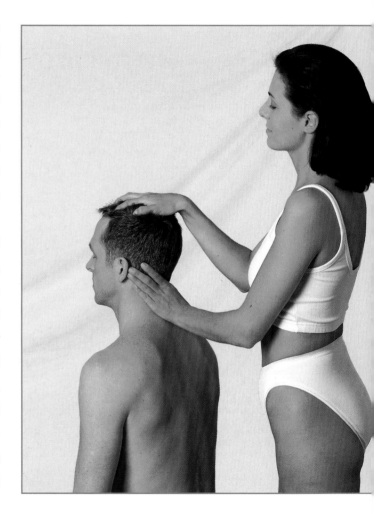

"Combing" the scalp
Your partner should sit comfortably in a chair that supports the lower back. Stand behind the chair and place your right hand on top of their head so that your fingertips are level with the hairline. Your left hand should support the head gently, with your middle fingertip level with the hairline behind the left ear, and your thumb on the other side level with the hairline behind the right ear. Using your right hand, "comb" the scalp with the tips of your fingers from the top of the head down to meet the other hand. Repeat the movement, starting further toward the sides of the head so that the whole of the head is massaged.

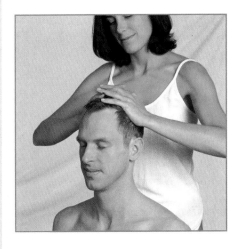

Using the heels of your hands

Place the heels of your hands above your partner's ears. Press gently, and slide your hands upward and over the top of the head so that they meet (as shown above). Place your hands back in the starting position but slightly farther round the back of the head, and repeat the movement. Repeat about four times, so that the whole of the head has been massaged. This stroke is marvellous for loosening the scalp – it literally lifts tension out of the head.

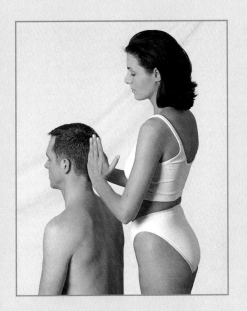

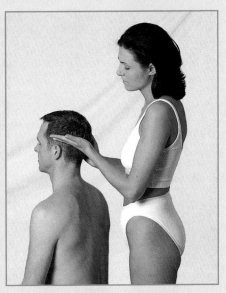

Using the edges of your hands

1 Place your right hand around the base of your partner's skull so that you are supporting their head. Using the outside edge of your left hand, slide it upward and downward around the whole of the back of the head.

2 Continue the movement over the top of the head. Your partner should eventually feel warmth and maybe a slight tingling sensation. Repeat the movement from side to side across the back and sides of the head and then change hands to continue.

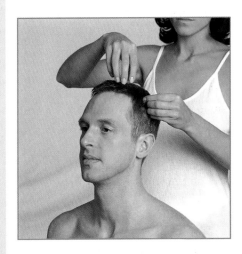

"Pinching" the head

Using both hands, pinch the scalp in short quick movements with the tips of your thumbs and fingers. If you wish you can actually pull the hair slightly as you do the movement. Repeat all over the head.

Self massage on the face

Receiving a massage can be a wonderful experience, but there will be times when it is not possible. However, you can easily massage yourself. This is a wonderful way of becoming more in tune with your own body, and because you know exactly where your aches and pains are, you will be more sensitive to your own needs. Giving yourself a face massage can improve your appearance because it increases circulation to the skin and generally freshens its appearance. A face massage can also ease headaches, relieve anxiety and eyestrain, and reduce facial tension.

You may like to use a little essential oil for an extra touch of luxury. If you have dry skin, use one drop of either rose, camomile, jasmine or neroli oil in a little avocado, apricot kernel or wheatgerm oil. For sensitive skin use one drop of rose, camomile or neroli oil in a little sweet almond, grapeseed or evening primrose oil. Lavender is sometimes helpful for sensitive skins, but always use it in a very low dilution of only one percent of the carrier or base oil. For oily skin use one drop of lavender, bergamot or geranium in a little grapeseed or apricot kernel oil. For mature skin use one drop of frankincense or neroli oil in a base oil of jojoba, wheatgerm, avocado or apricot kernel.

You can incorporate some of the following massage movements into your daily beauty routine, when applying a moisturizer or a nightcream.

Temple massage
Continue the same movements, using your middle fingers to massage your temples. This area often feels sensitive, so use just enough pressure without causing discomfort. Both forehead and temple massage are particularly soothing for headaches. You may like to use a little lavender or peppermint oil.

Forehead massage
(left) Place the pads of your index and middle fingers on your forehead between the hairline and eyebrows. Using small circular movements, massage the area while visualizing the tension being released from your head. Move your fingers up a little toward the hairline and repeat the circular movements.

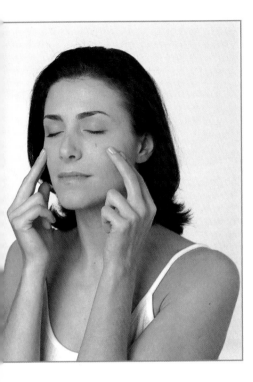

Cheek massage

Place the pads of your index and middle fingers on your cheekbones. Gently rotate your fingers in small circular movements over the whole cheek area. Tension often builds up in the cheeks from constant use of the muscles when we eat and speak. People who grate their teeth at night or clench their jaw are particularly prone to tension in the cheeks.

Thumb pressure under the eyebrows

Hook the pads of your thumbs under the inner edge of your eyebrows. It often helps to lean forward on a table to provide more pressure. Hold this position for about ten seconds and then repeat, five times in all. This is good for headaches and sinus problems.

Self massage on the hands

Hand massage can be done virtually anywhere and does not necessarily have to include the use of oil. Some people prefer to use an ordinary handcream. A lot of tension is stored in the muscles of your hands from carrying out daily activities such as picking up objects, holding on to the steering wheel of a car or handling money. By using some of the suggested hand-massage movements you will be counteracting any strain by "opening out" the palms and stretching the fingers.

Hand massage is a wonderful way of rounding off a manicure, or you could keep some handcream next to your bed and massage it into your hands last thing at night to soothe and relax them – the cream will nourish your skin while you sleep. For a really deep moisturizing effect, dilute one drop of rose or frankincense oil in about 2 teaspoons (10 ml) of wheatgerm oil. Massage the hands as shown for 10–15 minutes and then sleep in cotton gloves. Next morning your hands will feel wonderfully soft.

Thumb circling
This movement can be carried out almost anywhere, whether you are at home, in the office, or on a train. With the palm of your left hand facing upward, use the thumb of your right hand to make small circles. Repeat on the right hand with your left thumb. Hands are constantly being used with the fingers bent, and this movement helps to "open out" the hands and loosen any tension. You will also be energizing the many reflexology points in the hand.

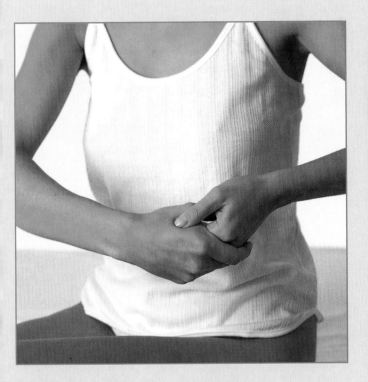

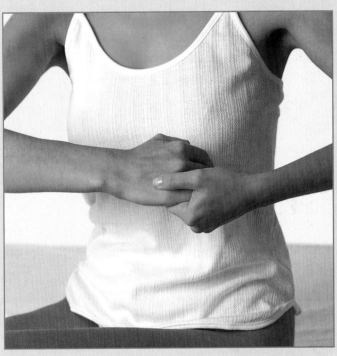

Thumb pressure on acupuncture points
Using fairly deep pressure, press your left thumb on the web between your right thumb and index finger. Hold for about ten seconds then release. This acupuncture point is usually quite sensitive, and pressing it can relieve headaches and migraines. Pressure here can also help with eye problems, neck and shoulder tension, colds, sore throats, toothache and fever.

Thumb sliding
Gently slide the thumb of your left hand between the tendons and bones of each finger on the right hand. Start just above the knuckle and slide up to the wrist, beginning at the little finger and working across to the thumb. Repeat on the left hand.

Finish your hand massage by holding in turn the base of each finger between the pads of the thumb and index finger of the other hand. Slide your thumb and index finger gradually to the tip. Pay particular attention to the fingertips and exert a little more pressure there to stimulate the nerve endings and increase energy to the body. Once you have completed the sequences on pages 132–3, hold your hands with the palms facing inward and about 2in (5cm) apart. Be aware of the energy between them and then bring them together as if praying. Feel the warmth of two hands gradually becoming one.

Prevention and healing

Cellulite, constipation and bloating

You don't have to be ill or suffering from aches and pains to reap the benefits of massage therapy. Massage will certainly help a range of ailments, but it can also prevent certain problems from occurring in the first place. Conditions such as cellulite, constipation, headaches and sinusitis are common nowadays, but you can help to prevent them by changing your lifestyle and diet. Remember also that by drinking plenty of water, preferably filtered or bottled, you will be helping your body to flush out any toxins and consequently increase its self-healing powers.

The massage sequences shown here can be performed without oil, with the exception of kneading and wringing. If you wish to use oil, choose one of the following: geranium, rosemary, fennel or juniper are good for cellulite; marjoram or rosemary are effective for constipation; fennel or peppermint work well for bloating. Headaches caused by tightness in the neck and shoulders, or by eyestrain, respond to lavender, peppermint or rosemary. Choose eucalyptus, peppermint or pine for sinus problems caused by congestion.

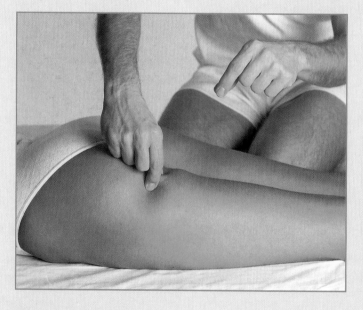

Cellulite (pinching)
Using your thumbs and index fingers, pick up the flesh in a series of quick, sharp pinching movements. Reddening of the skin shows increased circulation. Continue the movement over the whole thigh, hip and buttock area, using your hands alternately. Be careful not to pinch and squeeze for too long. Repeat on the other side.

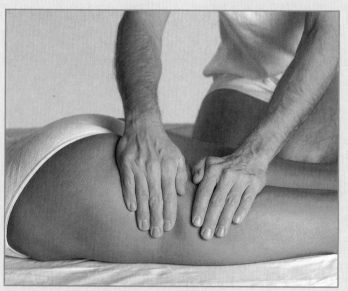

Cellulite (wringing)
Place your hands, palms down, on the upper thigh. Push and pull your hands in opposite directions so that the flesh is literally being "wrung". Repeat on the other thigh. This movement will increase the circulation to the area and help to dispose of any toxic build-up owing to a sluggish lymphatic system.

Constipation and bloating

1 (below) Kneel to the left of your partner level with their hips. Place your right hand on top of your left hand, palms facing downward, on your partner's abdomen, level with the right hip bone and about 2in (5cm) in toward the middle. This is where the ascending colon begins. Use your right hand to put pressure on your left hand. Press with your fingers pointing upward toward the ribs, then release. Continue the movement, gradually moving your hands up toward the area below the right side of the ribcage.

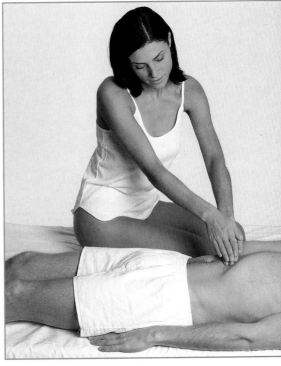

2 (above) Once you have reached the ribcage, turn your hands round so that they are facing horizontally across your partner's body. Continue to press and release all the way across to the other side of the ribcage. Then turn your hands so that they face downward and continue the movement down the descending colon, finishing on the opposite side from where you started. Repeat two to three times. These two stages follow the direction of the colon, or large intestine, helping to move energy along its pathway. The movement is useful for relieving abdominal gas, which can cause bloating.

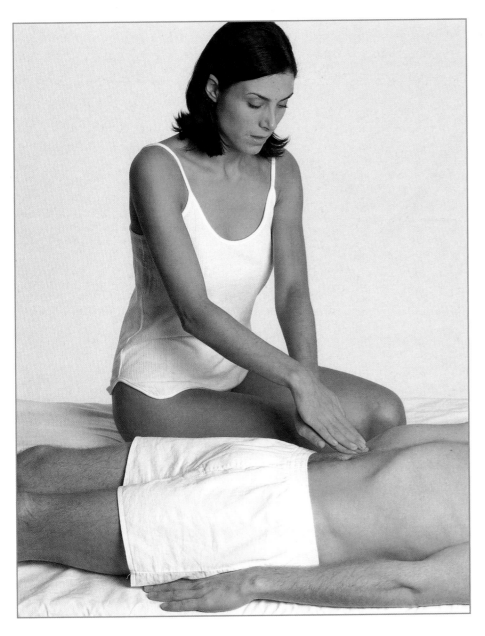

Headaches and sinusitis

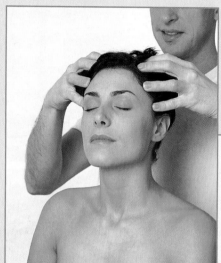

Headaches (tension in the neck and shoulders)

(below) Place your right hand across your partner's forehead for support, and the fingers of your left hand across the back of their head. Massage the scalp with the pads of your fingers, using small circular movements over the back of the head and down to the base of the skull. Change hands and repeat the movement. This is good for headaches caused by tightness in the neck and shoulders.

Headaches (eyestrain)

1 (above) Your partner should be sitting in a chair with their lower back supported. Stand behind the chair and place both your hands, with fingers apart, on either side of the top of the head. Using the same rotating movements with the pads of all your fingers, work all over the top and sides of the head as far forward as the hairline. Feel the scalp moving beneath your fingertips so that you release tension all over the area.

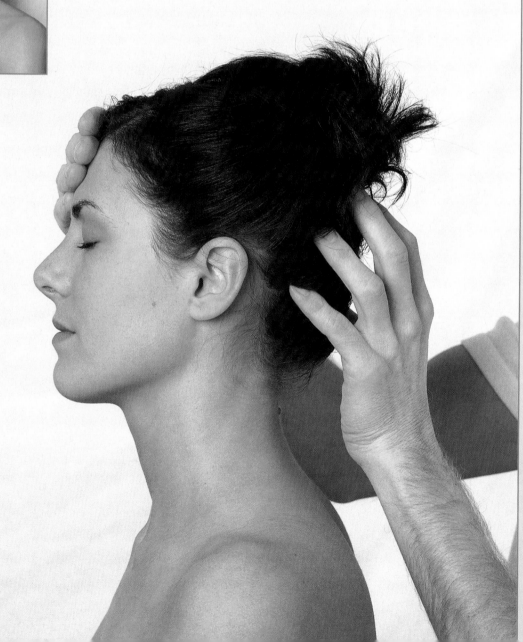

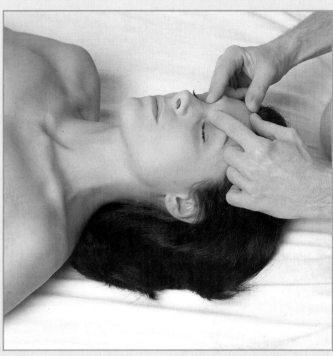

Sinusitis (thumb pressure)

Ask your partner to lie on their back and close their eyes. Place your thumbs in the middle of their forehead. Gently press down with the pads, not the nails, of your thumbs. Hold the pressure for a few seconds then release. Move your thumbs up the forehead a little, press and then release. Continue the movement so that your thumbs move gradually up to the hairline. Place your thumbs back at the starting position ready to repeat two to three times.

Sinusitis (finger pressure)

Place the pads of your index fingers just above the bridge of your partner's nose under the corners of the eyebrows. Steady their head by holding your other fingers on either side of the forehead. Using pressure with the index fingers, push upward under the brow bone and hold for about five seconds before releasing. Repeat the movement four to six times. People who suffer from regular sinus problems because of congestion will find this area quite sensitive. The movement also helps to relieve headaches resulting from sinus congestion.

Touch and holistic vision

The greatest sense in our body is our touch sense. It is probably the chief sense in the process of sleeping and waking; it gives us our knowledge of depth or thickness and form; we feel, we love and hate, are touchy and untouched, through the touch corpuscles of the skin.
J Lionel Taylor *The Stages of Human Life*, 1921, p157

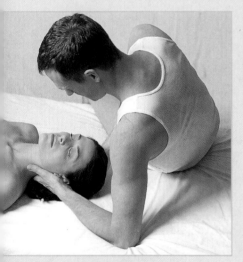

Once you have practised and mastered the massage sequences outlined in this book you will begin to realize that it is very much a two-way therapy between the giver and the receiver. For massage to be a truly holistic experience, the giver and the receiver should be in tune with one another. The giver should make the receiver feel really relaxed by focusing all their energy on the part of the body that they are massaging. Likewise the receiver should focus awareness on the area being massaged. This will help both partners to identify areas of tension and eliminate it through conscious thought and relaxation. It is almost as if both partners are massaging themselves from the inside out using visualization of energy. The giver will be massaging from the outside in, not just with the hands but by also visualizing a healing energy being transmitted or exchanged. Both partners should try to breathe slowly and deeply, or maybe even in harmony. The giver should emphasize the pressure of a stroke while breathing out. In this way both partners become centred and focused.

Try to eliminate all negative thoughts during a massage. Remember that energy tends to follow thought, so that wherever your attention is focused your inner energies will follow. If you allow your thoughts to drift away so that you are almost in a meditative state, your energies will be directed toward the body and its ability to heal itself. A lot of body tension is simply stored emotion – so be prepared for certain emotions to rise to the surface and don't be afraid to let them go.

With time you will become more intuitive and creative when giving a massage. There doesn't have to be a rigid structure, and each session will vary according to your partner's needs. Let your hands become your eyes. Some of the most skilled massage therapists are actually blind, having to rely on their hands to earn a living.

Massage is more than just a therapy, it is an art that allows tension and resistance to give way to pleasure – and there is no denying that touch fills a deep human need. Touch should be part of an holistic approach to health and a source of instinctive natural pleasure that we can benefit from throughout life. To touch someone in a gentle manner is saying that you care about them.

Through touch it is possible for one soul to reach out and touch another, thereby imparting a sense of peace and inner tranquillity.

Appendix: blending chart

As you become familiar with essential oils you will be able to experiment with blending them. A good combination of three oils includes one flower, one fruit and one herb. Another factor to consider is the intensity of the individual oils. For example, geranium, rose, frankincense, sandalwood and neroli all have a powerful aroma, so you may need to add only one drop to a blend.

This essential oil blending chart provides a useful guide to help you make your choice. Starting with the first oil on the chart, basil, simply slide your finger along the page to see with which oils it blends.

The chart was formulated by Paula Martin and Alan Crook and is part of a learning aid in the tuition of clinical aromatherapy at the Paula Martin School of Aromatherapy & Natural Therapies.

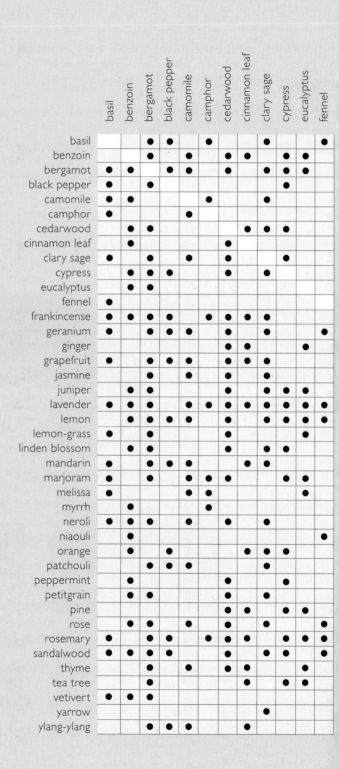

	basil	benzoin	bergamot	black pepper	camomile	camphor	cedarwood	cinnamon leaf	clary sage	cypress	eucalyptus	fennel
basil			●	●					●			●
benzoin			●		●		●	●				
bergamot	●	●		●	●				●	●	●	
black pepper	●		●						●			
camomile	●	●				●			●			
camphor	●				●							
cedarwood		●	●					●	●			
cinnamon leaf		●					●					
clary sage	●		●		●		●			●		
cypress		●	●	●			●					
eucalyptus		●	●									
fennel	●											
frankincense	●	●	●	●		●	●	●	●			
geranium	●		●	●	●		●		●			●
ginger							●	●			●	
grapefruit	●		●	●	●		●		●			
jasmine			●		●		●		●			
juniper		●	●				●		●	●	●	
lavender	●	●	●		●	●	●		●	●	●	●
lemon		●	●	●	●		●		●	●	●	
lemon-grass	●		●				●					
linden blossom		●	●				●					
mandarin	●		●	●	●				●	●		
marjoram	●		●		●		●			●	●	
melissa	●					●					●	
myrrh		●										
neroli	●	●	●			●						
niaouli	●											●
orange		●			●			●	●	●		
patchouli			●	●	●				●			
peppermint		●					●			●		
petitgrain		●	●				●					
pine							●	●			●	●
rose		●	●		●		●					●
rosemary	●		●	●		●	●	●		●	●	●
sandalwood	●	●	●	●			●			●	●	
thyme			●		●			●			●	
tea tree			●						●		●	●
vetivert	●	●	●									
yarrow									●			
ylang-ylang			●	●	●				●			

	frankincense	geranium	ginger	grapefruit	jasmine	juniper	lavender	lemon	lemon-grass	linden blossom	mandarin	marjoram	melissa	myrrh	neroli	niaouli	orange	patchouli	peppermint	petitgrain	pine	rose	rosemary	sandalwood	thyme	tea tree	vetivert	yarrow	ylang-ylang	
		•		•			•		•		•	•	•		•							•	•	•			•			basil
				•	•	•		•			•	•	•	•	•	•	•	•	•	•		•	•	•			•			benzoin
		•	•	•	•	•	•	•	•	•	•		•		•			•				•	•	•	•	•	•		•	bergamot
		•		•	•		•	•			•				•			•				•	•	•					•	black pepper
		•	•	•			•	•			•	•	•		•							•		•		•			•	camomile
	•						•				•	•	•	•						•										camphor
	•	•	•	•	•	•	•	•				•						•			•	•	•	•			•		•	cedarwood
	•	•	•	•							•				•		•	•				•	•				•		•	cinnamon leaf
	•	•	•	•	•	•	•	•				•			•			•				•		•		•		•		clary sage
					•	•	•	•	•			•						•		•		•	•	•		•				cypress
			•			•	•	•	•	•			•		•							•	•		•	•	•			eucalyptus
		•					•	•								•						•	•	•						fennel
		•	•	•	•	•	•	•	•		•		•	•			•	•		•		•	•		•	•				frankincense
	•		•	•	•	•	•	•	•		•		•		•							•	•	•		•				geranium
	•	•		•			•				•	•		•			•					•	•	•		•				ginger
	•	•	•		•	•	•	•			•	•		•			•			•		•	•			•			•	grapefruit
	•	•		•		•	•	•			•			•			•					•		•			•		•	jasmine
	•	•		•	•		•	•	•		•		•		•	•			•	•		•	•	•			•		•	juniper
	•	•	•	•	•	•		•	•	•	•	•	•		•	•	•	•	•	•	•	•	•	•	•	•	•		•	lavender
	•	•		•	•	•	•		•			•			•	•	•	•		•		•	•			•		•	•	lemon
		•		•	•	•	•					•			•	•	•		•			•				•		•		lemon-grass
		•	•	•	•		•	•	•						•					•		•		•					•	linden blossom
	•	•											•				•	•	•	•		•	•	•			•			mandarin
											•				•			•	•	•		•	•	•						marjoram
	•	•	•	•	•		•	•			•				•							•	•	•			•	•	•	melissa
	•														•			•				•		•						myrrh
		•	•		•		•	•			•	•						•	•			•	•	•					•	neroli
						•	•	•	•	•		•				•	•		•	•	•	•		•						niaouli
	•	•	•	•	•		•	•			•	•					•	•				•	•			•	•		•	orange
		•	•				•		•			•	•	•								•	•	•		•			•	patchouli
							•				•	•			•		•					•	•	•					•	peppermint
		•						•				•			•		•				•	•	•						•	petitgrain
	•					•	•	•							•		•	•	•			•		•	•					pine
	•	•	•	•	•	•	•	•		•	•		•		•		•			•		•		•			•		•	rose
	•	•	•		•	•	•	•	•		•	•			•	•	•	•	•			•		•	•	•	•	•	•	rosemary
	•	•	•		•		•	•			•	•	•		•			•		•	•	•		•		•			•	sandalwood
						•	•	•			•		•		•					•	•	•			•					thyme
	•		•		•	•	•	•	•		•	•			•					•	•	•		•						tea tree
	•	•	•	•	•		•								•	•				•		•	•					•		vetivert
						•		•	•			•										•								yarrow
		•	•			•	•		•		•	•		•		•		•		•		•		•			•			ylang-ylang

Index

Useful addresses

Massage Associations
UK: *The London College of Massage*
5 Newman Passage
London W1P 3PF
Tel: +44.171.3233574

USA: *American Massage Therapy Association*
820 Davis Street, Suite 100
Evanston
IL 60201-4444
Tel: +1.847.8640123
www.amtamassage.org

Canada: *Canadian College of Massage and Hydrotherapy*
5160 Yonge Street
North York
Ontario M2N 6L9
Tel: +1.416.2508690

Australia: *Association of Massage Therapists*
Level 1, 47 Spring Street
Bondi Junction
New South Wales 2022
Tel: +61.2.93692998

Aromatherapy Associations
UK: *International Federation of Aromatherapists*
Stamford House
24 Chiswick High Road
London W4 1TH
Tel: +44.181.7422606

USA: *The American Alliance of Aromatherapy*
PO Box 750428
Petaluma, CA 94975
Tel: +1.707.7786762

Canada: *Canadian National School of Aromatherapy*
2604 Hornsgate Drive
Mississauga
Ontario L5K 1P6
Tel: +1.905.8239581

Australia: *International Federation of Aromatherapists*
P.O. Box 2210
Central Park Vic. 3145
Tel: +61.3.98851643
Information: 1902240125

Essential Oil Suppliers
UK/Australia: *Aqua Oleum*
(Mail Order)
Unit 3, Lower Wharf
Wallbridge
Stroud, Glos GL5 3JA
Tel: +44.1453.753555

USA/Canada: *Aroma Vera*
3384 South Robertson Place
Los Angeles, CA 90034
Tel: +1.310.2800407
www.aromavera.com

A comprehensive directory of resources for massage and aromatherapy can be found on the Internet at:
www.fragrant.demon.co.uk

Acknowledgments

The publisher would like to thank the following people and photographic libraries for permission to reproduce their material.
t: top; c: centre; b: bottom;
l: left; r: right

page 10 Robert Harding Picture Library; page 15 DBP Archives; page 85tl The Garden Picture Library; page 85bl Images Colour Library; page 85tr The Photographers Library; page 85br Images Colour Library; page 86 The Garden Picture Library; page 87tr A–Z Botanical; page 87cr The Garden Picture Library; page 87br DBP Archives; page 92 Images Colour Library; page 93tr The Garden Picture Library; page 93cr DBP Archives; page 93br DBP Archives; page 98 The Photographers Library; page 99tr Robert Harding Picture Library; page 99cr Robert Harding Picture Library; page 99br DBP Archives; page 106 Images Colour Library; page 107tr DBP Archives; page 107cr DBP Archives; page 107br DBP Archives; page 112 Robert Harding Picture Library; page 112–13 Images Colour Library; page 114 Images Colour Library; page 115 Images Colour Library; page 116–17 Images Colour Library; page 117 Dan Lodge/Serpentine Editorial; page 118t Images Colour Library; page 118b Solo Syndication/Evening Standard; page 119 Solo Syndication/Evening Standard; page 120–1 Images Colour Library; page 121 Bridgeman Art Library/Victoria and Albert Museum; page 122 Superstock Ltd; page 122–3 Images Colour Library; page 126 Bridgeman Art Library/British Library; page 127 Robert Harding Picture Library.

All commissioned photography by Antonia Deutsch.